Gifted and Talented Children in the Regular Classroom

E. Paul Torrance, Emeritus

University of Georgia

and

Dorothy A. Sisk

Lamar University

Creative Education Foundation Press
Buffalo, New York

The Creative
Education
Foundation
Press®

Gifted and Talented Children
in the Regular Classroom

Project Coordinator: Grace Guzzetta, Director of Publications

Cover Design: Reilley Printing & Graphics

Art Direction: Michael J. Reilley & Domenic J. Licata

ISBN 0-930222-06-7

©1997
Creative Education Foundation Press
1050 Union Road
Buffalo, New York 14224

Table of Contents

Foreword

I am delighted to see this current work designed especially for the teacher of gifted and talented children in the regular classroom — prepared by two of the world's foremost leaders and pioneers in the areas of giftedness and creativity. It condenses in one book their wealth of background and experience in this field. These two extremely knowledgeable individuals also provide a very extensive bibliography for further study.

Paul Torrance needs no introduction. He has developed and introduced creative programs for gifted students for almost half a century, and is recognized world-wide for his accomplishments. His doctoral students have also pressed on with his teachings in every part of the world. Dorothy Sisk has been on the forefront of the gifted education and creativity movements ever since her appointment to head of the U.S. Office of Education's Office of Gifted and Talented in the 1970's. Since then, she too has gained world-wide recognition for her boundary-breaking work in this field.

I am heartened by the authors' belief that ". . . it is time we devise concepts and procedures which will engage the gifted and non-gifted in such a way that all children may attain their highest potential." They present such concepts and procedures in great detail — including Creative Problem-Solving (CPS) as the ". . . key to success of all of the other methods of instruction described in this book." In this regard, I have recently been redefining CPS as a "4th R" — reading, 'riting, 'rithmetic and "reframing" (my tentative word choice) — a fourth basic skill essential to all education. The meanings of the word "reframing" express or imply the full process of CPS: reviewing (Fact-Finding), re-defining (Problem-Finding), re-structuring (Idea-Finding), re-solving (Solution-Finding), re-doing (Acceptance-Finding).

Creativity might be considered an infinite continuum, along which each of us is forever able to progress. Interestingly, in working with students who are far up the continuum, we have found that they still seem to make great progress in pushing to new limits. It reminds me of Ralph Sockman's poetic expression, "The larger the island of knowledge, the longer the shoreline of wonder."

During many presentations to teachers of gifted students, I have been stressing, "You teach gifted children; in CPS programs, we teach for giftedness in children — from the mentally challenged to the gifted." Highly gifted students might well "turn off" or "turn out" — be lost or even prove dangerous, as the authors stress — if not challenged in the classroom. The authors now emphasize that average or below average students can also be "turned on" by challenging educational processes.

A conference-presenter once explained how she had been given responsibility for a class of gifted students, and found herself inventing many successful methods of challenging them to greater heights. Later, to her surprise, she found she was able to successfully use or adapt her invented methods for regular classroom students. That is what I hope all readers of this book will do.

All classroom teachers should be able to find significant help in this book in motivating all their students and in drawing more fully on each one's full potential. I fervently hope that each of you will be inspired by the authors to ever-more recognize and develop the unique 'potentials in each of your students. Hopefully, they will also help you discover ways to use the great strengths of each highly gifted student to mentor and otherwise help other students appreciate and nurture their own talents. Athletic giftedness has always been appreciated in this way.

Researchers and educators such as J. P. Guilford, Calvin Taylor and Howard Gardner have long stressed the value of learning to recognize multiple, diverse talents in students. This book will help you do that better, as well as understand and utilize these talents for the benefit of all your students. You can experience the joy of helping each one of them to ever-more appreciate and develop his or her potentials along that infinite continuum.

All the best to you in this great quest!

Sidney J. Parnes

Preface

The predominant way of educating gifted and talented children has always been in the regular classroom. After growing attempts since 1958 to establish special schools, special classes, and "pull-out" classes, research shows (Cox, Daniel & Boston, 1985) that gifted students are spending most of their instructional time in regular classroom settings. Viewing the scene in 1997, there seems to be an increased sentiment in favor of educating gifted and talented children in the regular classroom.

A similar condition seems to exist world-wide, despite the efforts of the World Council for Gifted and Talented Education and other such organizations. It is well-known that some of the more advanced nations have resisted separate programs for the gifted and talented. For example, Japan has taken a very strong stand against such programs. Of course, there are schools like the laboratory school at Nara University and private schools which are in fact schools for the gifted. Raina's (1996) survey reports that gifted and talented programs do not exist in some nations. While there has been an enormous increase world wide in gifted education and in gifted and talented programs, the evidence indicates that most gifted and talented children spend most of their time in the regular classroom.

The authors believe that it is time to devise concepts and procedures which will engage the gifted and non-gifted in such a way that all children may attain their highest potential. This is precisely what we have tried to do in this book. We have described methods of instruction that are capable of involving all children in putting forth their best efforts. We have also described devices which take children beyond learning and doing the things that they love and do best and giving those who need mentors these kinds of experiences.

The opening chapter makes an effort to show how recent breakthroughs in research concerning the human mind and personality have resulted in the emergence of a new and challenging concept of gifted-ness and talent. This concept stresses the importance of emphasis upon potentiality rather than upon norms and single measures of giftedness. It involves movement away from concepts of a single type of giftedness and talent, fixed intelligence and beliefs in predetermined development.

The second chapter considers the goals in teaching gifted and talented children. The authors are convinced that the creative energies of gifted children need to be activated and guided early, or else they will be lost — or prove dangerous. The concept of what teachers and experts regard as characteristics that should be encouraged and those which should be discouraged is discussed. Data from the early 1960's were compared with those obtained in 1995. The 1995 findings are even more encouraging than those from the early 1960's and indicate that the environment has become more favorable to creative development.

In the third chapter, the authors consider the consequences of the acceptance of a complex concept of giftedness and talent for the process of identification. This task is seen as searching for indications of unusual potentialities which, if given sound guidance and encouragement, can result in outstanding achievements of value to society. The importance of identification is discussed, and procedures and means of identification are described.

Chapter 4 examines the problem of motivating gifted and talented children to learn. New findings concerning abilities and the built-in motivation of certain methods of instruction are discussed. Major reasons for lack of motivation are identified and suggestions for avoiding them are given.

In Chapter 5, we have evaluated traditional curriculum practices for gifted and talented children, and new alternatives are suggested. Such promising curriculum frontiers as providing opportunities for self-initiated learning, emphasizing strengths, using academic disciplines as ways of thinking, providing a responsive environment, revising concepts of readiness, searching for one's uniqueness, opening up new frontiers, helping children develop an acceptance of limitations, changing empha-sis on sex roles, reducing the isolation of gifted students, encouraging gifted and talented children to find mentors, and developing a spirit of mission are suggested.

Chapter 6 on creative problem solving provides the key to the success of all the other methods of instruction described in this book. Creative abilities and the steps in the creative problem solving process are also offered. Several alternative approaches are identified and described. Some of the pitfalls of using creative problem solving are identified and described. Finally, some of the national and international programs and competitions are given.

Chapter 7 presents creative problem solving through role playing as a way of involving every child in a classroom at a deep level. This chapter shows how role playing involves both hemispheres of the brain, all of the modalities and intelligences. Some of the role playing production techniques for making learning more powerful are discussed. The steps in the process are described and discussed. Guidelines for using role playing in classroom learning are offered.

In Chapter 8, cooperative learning is presented as another device for involving all of the children in a classroom and enriching their experiences. Alternative models of cooperative learning are identified and evaluated. Cautions concerning the use of cooperative learning in the regular classroom are discussed. Research concerning cooperative learning is reviewed briefly.

Chapter 9 presents Torrance's Incubation Model of Teaching as another vehicle which is ideally suited to teaching gifted and talented children in the regular classroom. This three-stage model is described in some detail but a full description will be found in Torrance and Safter's book (1990), *The Incubation Model of Teaching.*

The Incubation Model was initially devised for use in teaching children to read creatively. However, since creative reading is so important in teaching gifted and talented children in the regular classroom, additional suggestions and procedures are described in Chapter 10. There are skills that need to be further developed. In this chapter, some of these skills are identified and ways of developing them are outlined and what it means to read creatively is explained. The importance of encouraging children to do something with what is read is emphasized.

The authors have long held that gifted and talented children should be taught the skills and concepts of finding out things as early as possible. We think this is true with regard to all children, but gifted children will be able to go much further than others. For this reason, they should be encouraged and permitted to work outside of the classroom at times. In Chapter 11, some promising developments are discussed, and a course taught by Torrance to gifted sixth graders is described and illustrated by specific examples in teaching historiography, descriptive research, and experimental research. More recent developments in teaching statistics to children and qualitative research methods are discussed briefly.

Although Chapter 4 was devoted to motivating gifted and talented children to learn, the authors decided to add another chapter primarily on some of the recent research on the motivation of gifted and talented children in the regular classroom. Sisk's study tells the story of a large scale three-year study of economically disadvantaged children in several diverse locations. At the beginning of the study, none of the children were nominated by their teachers or qualified for gifted programs in their school systems. At the end of the project, over fifty percent were qualified for their school systems' gifted program. The procedures of the project are described in Chapter 12.

Mentoring is one of the prime devices for meeting the needs of gifted and talented children beyond the classroom. The value of mentoring in the adult achievement of gifted and talented children is reported in Torrance's longitudinal study. The model of the mentoring process is described and illustrated by examples. Suggestions are given for recruiting and assigning mentors and for monitoring mentorship programs. The thirteenth chapter attempts to show how participating in a mentor program encourages students, teachers, mentors, and parents to join hands to forge a nurturing relationship between the mentor and mentee and between the family and the school.

The final chapter is devoted to the problem of becoming a teacher of gifted and talented children. We have characterized this process as a unique invention, and a process of creative thinking. This process is described. The major requirement of the teacher's invention are identified and discussed. The obstacles that threaten this invention are reviewed.

1

Problems Of Educating Gifted And Talented Children In The Regular Classroom

ANY TEACHERS, school administrators, counselors, school psychologists, and parents complain that there is no commonly accepted definition of giftedness, even among national and international authorities. When educational and civic leaders have pleaded for support of programs for educating teachers of gifted children or for appropriate educational programs for gifted children, many legislators opposed such support, arguing that not even the experts know how to identify those who are gifted. They contend, that if there is disagreement about identifying the gifted, it is futile to attempt to educate teachers especially for the gifted and to provide special kinds of educational opportunities for them.

The problem, strangely, is not that the experts do not know how to identify gifted children, nor even that there is any genuine disagreement among the national and international authorities. The truth is that we have been expanding our concept of giftedness and talent and that we have been learning an increasingly large number of ways of identifying a greater number of different kinds of giftedness and talent.

Another problem is that many of those who have sought support for programs for gifted children have had fixed notions about giftedness. In many cases, their ideas have been so patently erroneous that their proposals have not made sense to legislators and other would-be supporters. In some cases, these fixed ideas have centered around one type of giftedness, usually the type identified by an intelligence test and represented by the index known as the "IQ." Until recently, there has been little support for Paul Witty's (1951) definition of giftedness as "consistently superior performance in any socially useful endeavor." A similar definition was offered in a report to the federal Office of Gifted and Talented Education by De Haan and Havighurst (1961). They stated that a gifted child is one who is superior in some ability that can make him/her an outstanding contributor to the welfare and quality of living in the society (pp.15).

Others have been over concerned about the degree of giftedness and have argued that the gifted must have IQ's of 180, 150, 140, or some other figure. From arguments around this point, there has arisen a great deal of confusing terminology, such as "genius," "highly gifted," "extremely gifted," "moderately gifted," "talented," and the like. Other arguments have centered around the fixity of the intelligence quotient.

Generally, however, serious students of the problem of educating gifted and talented children agree that our expanding knowledge makes it clear that the problem is complex, but not necessarily confusing. It is quite clear that there is a variety of kinds of giftedness and talent that should be cultivated, and they are not ordinarily cultivated without special efforts. It is also clear that if we establish a level on some single measure of giftedness, we eliminate many extremely gifted individuals on other measures of giftedness. It is also clear that intelligence may increase or decrease, at least in terms of available methods of assessing it, depending upon a variety of physical and psychological factors both within the individual child and within his/her environment.

The complexity engendered by our expanding knowledge of the human mind and its functioning should be exciting and challenging rather than confusing. The authors hope that the reader will find it so because this is the nature of things as teachers and parents experience them in trying to educate gifted and talented children. Furthermore this complex view of the nature of giftedness permeates this book. The authors hope that it will help the reader feel more comfortable, yet excited and challenged, in his/her efforts to teach gifted and talented children in elementary or high-school classrooms.

CHALLENGE OF A COMPLEX
VIEW OF GIFTEDNESS

The acceptance of a realistically complex view of the human mind is itself a tremendous advance. In moving from an oversimplified (and patently erroneous) view of giftedness and talent to a more complex one, we have reached a position where we can avoid many of the errors of the past. We should be able to develop a more humane kind of education for gifted and talented children — one in which these children will have a better chance to achieve their potentialities.

This more complex view of giftedness and talent is causing us to reevaluate many of the classical experiments upon which we have built educational practices. From this reexamination, it is becoming clear that children should be provided opportunities for mastering a variety of learning and thinking skills according to a variety of methods and that the outcomes of these efforts should be evaluated in a variety of ways. It will be one of the purposes of this book to illustrate some of this variety of learning and thinking skills, methods of learning, and evaluation procedures.

It is to be hoped that young teachers, as well as experienced educational leaders, will not be impatient with the complexity or the incompleteness of knowledge about giftedness. We do not yet know the end of the complexity of the functioning of the human mind and personality. This book, however, is inspired by the conviction that it is high time that we begin developing the strategies, methods, and materials that have built into them an acceptance of this complexity. In large part, it is derived from the authors and their associates' experimental work with gifted and talented children.

In their own studies of creative giftedness, the authors have continued to be increasingly impressed by the wonderful complexity of this single aspect of a person's intellectual functioning. Many fascinating insights concerning the functioning of children's minds occur even when we limit ourselves to the examination of such qualities of thinking as fluency of ideas, spontaneous flexibility, originality, and elaboration. Some children are exceptionally fluent in the production of ideas expressed in words but are unable to express ideas in figural or auditory symbols. Others may be tremendously fluent in expressing ideas in figural form but appear paralyzed mentally when asked to express them in words or sounds. Similar phenomena seem to occur when we consider creative movement or kinesthetic behavior.

A child may not be able to express his/her ideas verbally, visually, or any other way with a great deal of fluency and yet be quite gifted in other kinds of constructive, creative behavior. The child may produce a small number of ideas, but each idea may be quite original or unusual and of high quality. The child may be able to take a single idea and do an outstanding job of elaborating or expanding it, or he/she may produce ideas which show a great deal of flexibility of thinking.

The complexity of children's creative thinking does not end here. A child might respond quite creatively to one task and barely respond to another. For example, some children show tremendous originality and elaboration on the Incomplete Figures Test and respond very poorly to the Circles Test and vice versa (Torrance, 1962a). The Incomplete Figures Test confronts the child with incomplete structures, and this produces tension in most observers, making them want to complete the structures and integrate or synthesize their relatively unrelated elements. The pages of circles of the Circles Test, however, confront the subject with "perfect structures." In order to produce pictures and objects which have as a major part a circle, the child has to disrupt or destroy these "perfect structures," the circles. In the creative process, there seems to be an essential tension between the two opposing tendencies symbolized by these two tasks: the tendency toward structuring and synthesizing and the tendency toward disruption and diffusion of energy and attention. Most children seem able to express both tendencies with equal skill, but others seem able to express only one of these tendencies to any great degree.

The authors have mentioned here only a few of the ways that have been devised for measuring the mental abilities involved in creative thinking, yet we realize that we have only begun to represent psychometrically the different ways children can express their creative giftedness.

Anderson (1960) states that ability level can be thought of in terms of thresholds, and questions can be asked about the amount of the ability necessary to accomplish a task. Then consideration can be given to the factors that determine function beyond this threshold. There are cutoff points of levels about which the demonstration of ability in relation to minimum demands is determined by other factors. In other words, the creative-thinking abilities might show their differential effects only beyond certain minimal levels of intelligence.

To test this possibility, Yamamoto (1964), in one of the Minnesota studies of creative thinking reanalyzed the data from six of the partial replications already mentioned. In each case, students who scored in the top 20 per cent on the test of creative thinking were divided into three groups according to IQ (above 130, 120 to 129, and below 120). In general, the achievement of the first two groups did not differ from each other but was significantly higher than that of the third group (IQ below 120). This finding supports suggestions made previously by several people (MacKinnon, 1961; Roe, 1960; Torrance, 1962a).

Still almost unnoticed by educators is that part of the Getzels-Jackson study (1962) dealing with two kinds of psychosocial excellence or giftedness — that is, high social adjustment and high moral courage. It was found that just as the highly intelligent student is not always highly creative, the highly adjusted student is not always highly moral. Further, it was found that although the highly moral students achieved at a higher level than the highly adjusted students, the teachers perceived the highly adjusted students as the leaders rather than the highly moral ones. This is especially significant in a peer-oriented culture such as we have in the United States. It is well to recognize the dangers of giving rewards to those who accept the peer-value system and adjust almost automatically to the immediate group, almost without reference to moral values.

SOME OF THE SCIENTIFIC BASES OF GIFTEDNESS AND TALENT

AWAY FROM CONCEPTS OF A SINGLE KIND OF GIFTEDNESS AND TALENT

Many educators and psychologists have been struggling for years to tear themselves away from concepts of a single type of giftedness. Undoubtedly, this struggle has been motivated by vague anxieties that such concepts lead to errors and inhumane treatment for many children. The difficulty has been in finding a way to conceptualize the various kinds of intellectual giftedness and to develop measures of the different kinds of mental abilities involved. There have been numerous brave, but unsuccessful, attempts. For example, on the basis of the report of the Norwood Committee in England (Burt, 1958), the Education Act of 1944 in that country gave recognition to the hypothesis that there are different kinds of intellectual giftedness. Burt, in fact, maintains that the Education Act of 1944 assumes that children differ more in quality of ability than in amount. This act recommended a classification of secondary school, based on the idea that there are three main types of giftedness: a literary or abstract type to be educated at grammer schools, a mechanical or technical type to be educated at technical schools, and a concrete or practical type to be educated at modern schools. Burt argues that this scheme has not worked out as well as had been hoped. This may well be due, however, to still another oversimplification of the problem. Many believe, nevertheless, that this tripartite system in England is much more successful than earlier systems based on a single type of giftedness.

Guilford's Structure of Intellect (1956, 1959) and research related to the creative thinking or divergent production abilities have been especially effective in directing educators and psychologists away from their

Figure 1-1. Guilford's Structure of Intellect Model (From J. P. Guilford and R. Hoepfner, Current Summary of Structure Factors and Suggested Tests. Los Angeles: University of Southern California, 1963.)

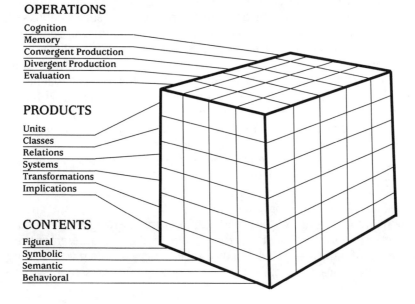

OPERATIONS

Cognition
Memory
Convergent Production
Divergent Production
Evaluation

PRODUCTS

Units
Classes
Relations
Systems
Transformations
Implications

CONTENTS

Figural
Symbolic
Semantic
Behavioral

dependence upon a single measure of giftedness. Guilford has given us what amounts virtually to a periodic table of different kinds of intelligence. His theoretical model of the structure of intellect has three dimensions: operations, contents, and products.

In this model the operations are the major kinds of intellectual activities or processes, the things that the organism does with the raw materials of information. The first, *cognition*, includes discovery, awareness, recognition, comprehension, or understanding. The second, *memory*, refers to retention or storage, with some degree of availability of information. Then there are two types of *productive thinking* in which something is produced from what has been cognized or memorized: *divergent production*, or the generation of information from given information, where emphasis is upon variety and quantity of output from the same source, and *convergent production*, or the generation of information where emphasis is upon achieving unique or conventionally accepted best outcomes (the given information fully determines the response). The fifth operation is *evaluation*, reaching decisions or making judgments concerning the correctness, suitability, adequacy, desirability, and so forth of information in terms of criteria of identity, consistency, and goal satisfaction.

These five operations act upon each of the kinds of content (figural, symbolic, semantic, and behavioral) and products (units, classes, systems, transformations, and implications).

In this book, the term *productive thinking* will be used to refer to what Guilford has defined as *convergent production* and *divergent production*. The term *creative thinking* will be used to refer to such abilities as fluency (large number of ideas), flexibility (variety of different approaches or categories of ideas), originality (unusual, off-the-beaten track ideas), elaboration (well developed and detailed ideas), sensitivity to defects and problems, and redefinition (perceiving in a way different from the usual, established, or intended way or use). *Measured creative thinking ability* will be used to refer to test scores which have been devised to assess these abilities.

Guilford and his associates' monumental work remained almost totally neglected by educators until Getzels and Jackson (1962) showed that highly creative or divergent thinking adolescents achieved as well as their highly intelligent peers, in spite of the fact that their average IQ was 23 points lower. Since at least 1898, psychologists have been producing instruments for assessing the creative-thinking abilities, making pleas for using such measures to supplement intelligence tests and recommending educational changes needed to develop creative talent (Torrance, 1962a). In the main, these earlier efforts to generate interest in creative development and other types of intellectual functioning not represented by intelligence tests were ignored or soon forgotten. Many of these earlier efforts are receiving attention now.

Meeker (1969) has shown how differential intellectual assessment can by means of a derived Structure of Intellect (SOI) profile give meaning and validity to academic expectancy. The differential assessments of the

SOI have curricular implications because they represent guidelines within the Guilford theory of intelligence. When teachers are provided with individual SOI profiles, they can construct individual programs for development and remediation.

The SOI diagnostic approach to teaching has a beneficial effect on self concept because they offer specific parameters for material to develop and enhance abilities.

The Guilford model is a complex information-processing model, yet Mary and Bob Meeker have demonstrated that the model can be applied to assessment and then used to organize instruction so that all children can receive practice in all of the major operations.

In selecting materials for this book, a serious effort has been made to provide ideas that can be used in teaching gifted and talented children in both regular and segregated classrooms. The ideas presented have almost infinite possibilities for use with a variety of types of gifted and talented children. It is to be expected that in the hands of some groups of gifted and talented children the line of development from these methods and materials will be quite different from what will occur in less gifted and talented groups. These materials and methods rarely require that specific questions be answered in a given way. It is to be hoped that teachers will not give severe disapproval when children answer questions or offer solutions to problems in a different way or ask different, more penetrating questions. Such questions and solutions are essential in many kinds of gifted performance.

Single studies such as those of Getzels and Jackson (1962) always leave many questions unanswered. Since the Getzels-Jackson data were obtained from a single school, one with an unusually large number of gifted students, their study did not tell us under what conditions their results could be anticipated. Torrance (1962a) and his associates have undertaken fifteen partial replications of the Getzels-Jackson study, hoping to obtain some clues to answer this question. In ten of these studies, the results have been essentially the same as in the Getzels-Jackson study. In the other five, the high IQ group scored significantly higher than the highly creative group on tests of achievement. In general it was Torrance's impression that the children in these five schools were taught primarily by methods of authority and had very little chance to use their creative-thinking abilities in acquiring educational skills. The average IQ was lower than in the schools where the Getzels-Jackson results were confirmed. These observations suggested that the phenomena Getzels and Jackson report may occur only in schools where students are taught in such a way that they have a chance to use their creative-thinking abilities in acquiring traditional educational skills or where the average IQ in the entire school is rather high.

It was observed that the highly creative pupils in at least two of the five schools overachieved in the sense that their educational quotients were considerably higher than their intelligence quotients. Thus, we thought that an ability gradient might be operating. According to the concept of the ability gradient suggested by J. E. Anderson (1960), ability level can be thought of in terms of thresholds, and questions can be asked about the amount of the ability necessary to accomplish a task. Then consideration can be given to the factors that determine function beyond this threshold. There are cutoff points of levels about which the demonstration of ability in relation to minimum demands is determined by other factors. In other words the creative thinking abilities might show their differential effects only beyond certain minimal levels of intelligence.

To test this possibility, Yamamoto (1964) in one of the Minnesota studies of creative thinking, reanalyzed the data from six of the partial replications already mentioned. In each case, students who scored in the top 20 per cent on the test of creative thinking were divided into three groups according to IQ (above 130, 120 to 129, and below 120). In general, the achievement of the first two groups did not differ from each other but was significantly higher than that of the third group (IQ below 120). This finding supports suggestions made previously by several people (MacKinnon, 1961; Roe, 1960; Torrance, 1962a).

NEW CONCEPTS OF MENTAL FUNCTIONING AND INTELLIGENCE

Two major recent concepts of mental functioning and intelligence have revolutionized the way we think of giftedness and talent. These new concepts are based on findings concerning hemisphericity, the specialized functions of the right and left hemispheres of the brain and the findings concerning multiple intelligences. In this chapter, the authors will present an overview concerning these concepts, and in later chapters we shall discuss specific implications for teaching gifted and talented children in the regular classroom.

The brain hemispheric theory maintains that people have two ways of processing information: linearly (using language and logic) and holistically (using nonverbal, visual, and kinesthetic modes). These specialized functions have been delineated in many sources (e.g. Buzan, 1991; Gazzaniga, 1988; Herrmann, 1987; Ornstein, 1973; Schmeck, 1988; Torrance, 1988; & Williams, 1983). These two ways of processing information can be expressed in terms of the ways in which left-dominant and right dominant persons approach problem-solving (Torrance, 1988).

BRAIN-HEMISPHERE THEORIES
Left-Dominant Individuals

They tend to be *conforming* persons and prefer structured assignments in which they can discover systematically by recalling verbal material.

Left dominant individuals look for specific facts that will sequence ideas in the form of an outline from which to draw conclusions and/or solve problems logically, in order to improve something.

Right-Dominant Individuals

They tend to be nonconforming persons who prefer open-ended assignments in which they can discover through exploration. They recall spatial imagery in order to look for main ideas that will show relationships in the form of a summary. From this summary they can produce ideas to solve problems intuitively to invent something new.

These two styles of processing information have also been translated into learning styles by numerous authors (e.g., Gregorc, 1979; Kolb, 1986, 1988; McCarthy, 1987; Torrance, 1988). From these learning styles they and others have developed ways of instruction that will involve all students and give them a chance to use their best abilities. For example, McCarthy (1987) combined the findings of the preceding theories and formed a new synthesis of the following four styles of learners: innovative, analytic, commonsense, and dynamic. The innovative learner seeks meaning through personal involvement and learns through discussion. He or she perceives information concretely, processes it randomly, and thinks divergently. The analytic learner values facts and the opinions of experts. Information is perceived abstractly and processed reflectively. This learner thrives in the traditional classroom. The commonsense learner wants to know how things work and seeks relevance. This person makes practical solutions. The dynamic learner is a risk taker who is interested in hidden possibilities. This person is a good problem solver and likes to make things happen.

This format concept has been translated into lesson plans and educational materials that will provide every student a chance to learn according to the method that will use his/her best abilities, learning and thinking style. McCarthy believes that every lesson should be taught in such a way that all students can succeed.

Several investigators developed measures of hemisphericity and learning preference. However, educators lack the competence to use the neurological measures or indicators and have steered away from them; they have shown a preference for the self-report measures based upon hemisphericity theory. The most frequently used of these are the instruments developed by Herrmann (1988), Kolb (1985), and Torrance (1988). Hermann's instrument is based on the quadrant concept (left cerebral hemisphere, right cerebral hemisphere, left limbic, and right limbic). Herrmann has developed a thorough training in the administration, interpretation, and use of his instrument. Kolb also uses a quadrant approach and defines them in terms of perceiving and processing. The quadrants describe four types of people based on their learning styles: divergers, assimilators, convergers, and accommodators. Torrance's instrument, known as *Style of Learning and Thinking* (SOLAT), is based on knowledge about thought processes that are identified with the functions of the left and right hemispheres of the brain. The SOLAT describes people as right, left, or whole-brained in their style of learning and thinking. Teaching procedures have been developed on the basis of identifications based on each of these instruments.

MULTIPLE INTELLIGENCES

More recently the multiple intelligences concept has caught the attention of educators, as well as the general public and at the present time is dominating the thinking of educators and development of educational materials. Although many investigators had been finding that there are a number of kinds of mental abilities, it was not until Howard Gardner's *Frames of Mind* (1983) came along that this concept received much attention. In Gardner's Theory of Multiple Intelligences, he argues that human beings have evolved to be able to carry out at least seven separate forms of analysis:

1. Linguistic intelligence (as a poet or other type of writer or speaker);
2. Logical-mathematical intelligence (as in a scientist);
3. Musical intelligence (as in a composer);
4. Spatial intelligence (as in a sculptor or airplane pilot);
5. Bodily-kinesthetic intelligence (as in an athlete or dancer);
6. Interpersonal intelligence (as in a salesman or teacher);
7. Intrapersonal intelligence (exhibited by individuals with accurate views of themselves).

(See note at end of chapter)

Since 1983, Gardner has further elaborated and developed these concepts through several books such as *Multiple Intelligences: The Theory in Practice* (1993). Gardner's concepts have attracted the attention of educators who are searching for more comprehensive and individualized educational systems. Many authors have translated these concepts into instructional and assessment materials. Examples of their products include the following:

- Thomas Armstrong. (1993). *Seven Kinds of Smart: Developing Your Many Intelligences.*
- Teresa Benzwie. (1995). *A Moving Experience.* (1996). *More Moving Experience.*
- E. Brewer and B. G. Campbell. (1991). *Rhythms of Learning: Creative Tools for Lifelong Learning.*
- Linda Campbell, Bruce Campbell, and Dee Dickinson. (1996). *Teaching and Learning through Multiple Intelligences.*

- Marilyn Coffin. (1996). *Team Science: Organizing Classroom Experiments that Develop Group Skills.*
- Daniel Goleman. (1996). *Emotional Intelligence.*
- David Lazear. (1994a). *Seven Pathways of Learning: Teaching Students and Parents about Multiple Intelligence.*
- (1994b). *Multiple Intelligence Approach to Assessment: Solving the Assessment Conundrum.* (1996). *Step Beyond Your Limits.*
- Douglas M. McPhee. (1996). *Limitless Learning: An Everyday Event.*
- Robert E. Myers. (1994). *Facing the Issues: Creative Strategies for Probing Critical Social Concerns.* (1996). *Cognitive Connections: Multiple Ways of Thinking with Math.*
- Robert E. Myers and E. Paul Torrance. (1994). *What Next? Futuristic Scenarios for Creative Problem Solving.*
- Laura Rose. (1996). *Developing Intelligences Through Literature.*

This is only a small sampling of multiple intelligences educational materials. It will be noted that some of the products deal with the whole gamut of multiple intelligences while others deal with one of the seven abilities or pathways of learning. The key author in this development has been David Lazear. Many educators have complained about the failure of Howard Gardner to provide methods of identification and evaluation of achievement. Lazear (1994b) has offered methods of handling both of these kinds of assessment. These suggestions depend primarily on observations of performances and the evaluations of products. Doubtless there will be further developments concerning this important matter.

STERNBERG'S TRIARCHIC MIND: A NEW THEORY OF INTELLIGENCE

Robert Sternberg (1988) has developed a new concept of intelligence which he calls "The Triarchic Mind" and this theory is attracting much attention.

As an elementary school pupil, Sternberg realized that something was wrong with intelligence testing. He did very poorly on intelligence tests, was confused by them, and never got very far in responding to them. He began doing research on intelligence tests. In the seventh grade, he was assigned a research project and chose to do it on intelligence tests. He administered the Stanford-Binet to his classmates and constructed his own intelligence test and administered it. This came to the attention of the principal, but his teacher defended him. However, the principal had the Stanford-Binet and other tests placed where children could not have access to them.

Sternberg continued his interest in the concept of intelligence through college, graduate school, and in his professional life as an educational psychologist. He is critical of four of the basic assumptions underlying most intelligence tests. These assumptions are:

1. To be quick is to be smart.
2. The highly verbal reads everything with great care and comprehension.
3. You can tell how smart a person is by the size of his/her vocabulary.
4. Intelligent people solve problems in the same way as less intelligent people, but better.

Sternberg (1988) believes that "intelligence is a quality that we use continually in our everyday lives — on the job, in our interpersonal relationships, in decision-making," (pp. x.) He maintains that traditional intelligence tests measure only a narrow spectrum of these skills. Further, he believes that intelligence must be examined in terms of three manifestations or aspects:

1. Its relationship to the internal world of the individual,
2. Its relationship to the external world of the individual, and
3. Its relationship to experience.

Sternberg illustrates the three manifestations of his triarchic theory with three profiles of intelligence. Alice came to Yale with outstanding test scores, college grades, and letters of recommendation. Her excellent critical abilities earned her outstanding grades during her first two years at Yale. After her first two years, she was no longer so outstanding, when it came to coming up with her own ideas and figuring out ways of implementing them. Alice was "IQ test smart" but not so distinguished in the synthetic, or practical, areas of intelligence.

Barbara's profile is in sharp contrast to Alice's. She entered Yale with good grades but abysmal aptitude test scores. Her letters of recommendation were superlative. They described her as an exceptionally creative student who designed and implemented creative research with only minimal supervision. Her resume showed her to have been actively involved in important research.

Celia appeared to be somewhere between Alice and Barbara. She was good on almost every measure of success but not truly outstanding on any. She proved to be outstanding, but in a different way from Alice and Barbara. Her expertise was in figuring out and adapting to the demands of the environment. She knows exactly what to do to get ahead. She excels in practical intelligence.

The Sternberg Multidimensional Abilities test was designed to measure the three kinds of intelligence and will be published by the Psychological Corporation. It will be appropriate for all ages from five years through adult. Separate scores will be provided for three kinds of item content: verbal (word-based problems), quantitative (number-based problems), and figural (form-based problems). Separate scores will also be obtainable for each of the three main parts of the triarchic theory: components of intelligence, coping with novelty and automatization (two separate subscores), and practical intelligence. The test will be in paper-and-pencil, multiple-choice format and suitable for group administration.

REALISTIC CONSIDERATION OF EDUCATING GIFTED AND TALENTED CHILDREN IN THE REGULAR CLASSROOM

Another new trend has been to educate gifted and talented children in the regular classroom. This requires more than enrichment and more than what has gone on in the typical regular classroom. In this changed concept, both gifted and talented children are identified and a deliberate attempt is made to meet their needs as well as all the other children who make up the regular classroom.

Educators have been slow to face this problem realistically. However, recently at least two excellent contributions have emerged by Renzulli (1994) and Winebrenner (1992). Renzulli's *School for Talent Development: A Practical Plan for Total School Improvement* is concerned with schoolwide improvement and Winebrenner concentrates on strategies and techniques for meeting the academic needs of the gifted and talented children in the regular classroom.

Renzulli also presents a variety of his inventions for meeting the complex needs of gifted and talented children. Among these invention are the total talent portfolio, curriculum compacting, the multiple menu model, the enrichment triad model, and the revolving-door model of identification.

Winebrenner's plan rests on the belief that gifted and talented children can identify themselves. She, too, recommends curriculum compacting and illustrates how this can be done for specific subjects such as math, geography, language arts, spelling, reading, literature, science, and social studies. She describes the use of learning contracts, the creation of more challenging activities, cooperative learning, and cluster groups.

AWAY FROM CONCEPTS OF FIXED INTELLIGENCE

From time to time investigators have assaulted the concept of fixed intelligence. Despite this, the view that intelligence is a capacity fixed once and for all by genetic inheritance is still held quite widely. Indeed, a great deal of empirical evidence seems at first glance to support the idea of fixed intelligence. However, Hunt (1961) proposed alternative explanations and summarized evidence that undermines this hypothesis.

It has been shown that performance scores (not IQ) on the Binet-type intelligence tests improves with age. Age-discrimination, however, was one of the criteria Binet used in selecting items. Although Binet (1909) regarded intelligence as "plastic," the fact that performance on tests selected on age-discrimination criteria showed improvement with age has been used to conclude that development is predetermined by genetic inheritance. Another argument has been that individual children show considerable constancy from one intelligence test to another. Since all intelligence tests traditionally have been validated against the Binet-type test, this is to be expected. It has also been shown that there are high intercorrelations among the various Binet-type tests, and this has been presented as evidence in favor of a high "g" (general ability) factor. Another argument of the adherents of fixed intelligence has been based on evidence that shows that intelligence tests are fairly good predictors of school achievement. Since curricula and achievement tests have been based on the intelligence-test concept of the human mind, this too is to be expected.

Studies involving hereditary versus environmental determination also have been used to support the idea of fixed intelligence. The evidence here, however, frequently has not supported the idea of fixed intelligence. Both hereditary and environmental influences interact in determining mental growth and educational achievement.

Hunt (1961) has summarized evidence from studies of identical twins reared apart, from repeated testing of the same children in longitudinal studies, and from studies of the effects of training or guided, planned learning experiences. He believes that studies of the constancy of the IQ within individuals pose the most serious challenge to fixed intelligence. These include studies both of stability with which individuals maintain their positions within a given group of individuals from one testing to another testing and of the variations of IQ within specific individuals.

Studies of the effects of schooling have been fairly convincing. Out of a group of people tested at some earlier age, those who complete the most schooling show the greatest increases and fewest decreases in IQ. Hunt cites studies by Lorge (1945), Vernon (1948), and deGroot (1948, 1951). In the area of early environmental influences, Hunt mentions the sustained work of Wellman, Skeels, and their colleagues of the Iowa group. This group continued their studies over many years, demonstrating many of the effects of training at the kindergarten and nursery level. The studies of Spitz (1945, 1946) have been quite influential in convincing psychiatrists and social caseworkers that intelligence is plastic and modifiable, not fixed and that mothering is crucial during the early years of life. Children deprived of social interaction or mothering fail to develop naturally either physically or mentally.

AWAY FROM BELIEFS IN
PREDETERMINED DEVELOPMENT

Long-standing beliefs in predetermined development have been used frequently to support the concept of fixed intelligence. Much evidence, however, indicates that deprivation of experience makes a difference in rates of various kinds of growth. The more severe the deprivation of experiences has been, the greater has been the decrease in the rates of development.

Arguments concerning inherited patterns of mental growth have also been placed in doubt by the work of Hunt (1961), Ojemann (1948), Ojemann and Pritchett (1963), and others. The evidence seems to indicate that intellectual development is quite different when children are exposed to guided, planned learning experiences from that which occurs when they encounter only what the environment just happens to provide.

This has led to the suggestion that educational programs should be based upon guided, planned experiences which in turn are based upon an analysis of the requirements of the learning task and the condition of the child. Analysis of the task must include a consideration of the structure of the task, possible strategies or processes by which the task can be achieved (alternative ways of learning, kinds of discriminations to be made, and so forth), and the settings or conditions which facilitate or impede achievement of the task (cultural, social, physical, and the like). Analysis of the child's condition should consider the stage of development relevant to the concepts or skills to be learned, the level of relevant abilities, especially the most highly developed ones (memory, logical reasoning, originality, judgments of space, and so forth), and the individual child's preferred ways of learning. The concern is with potentiality rather than norms. Examples of such educational experiences will be outlined in the section on classroom procedures.

In recent years new evidence has been provided to show that both intelligence and creativity can be changed (Wenger, 1987, 1992) and Torrance (1972a, 1979). Wenger suggests the following means for improving intelligence: weight control; abstinence of drugs, tobacco, and alcohol; special nutrients (Vitamin E); early reading and various games, image streaming and visualizing; and various other similar methods. Torrance has summarized the results of several hundred experiments showing that training in creative problem solving, participation in creative dramatic experiences or in curricular changes as in the Imagi/Craft materials by Cunnington and Torrance (1965) result in significant change. Marilyn Ferguson (1973) and other writers have also indicated these changes in intelligence and creativity.

Sternberg (1983) has written a small book on how to teach intelligence in which he concludes that we do indeed need intervention programs for training students in intellectual skills. He points out that we have witnessed an unprecedented decline in the intellectual skills of our students as evidenced by declines in Scholastic Aptitude (SAT) scores. He believes that we now have available a number of programs that are effective and accomplishing this. He discusses such programs as teaching the components of intelligence, instrumental enrichment, philosophy for children, and the Chicago mastery learning in reading.

CONCLUSION

In this chapter an effort has been made to show how recent breakthroughs in research concerning the human mind and personality and their functioning have resulted in the emergence of a new and challenging concept of giftedness and talent. This concept stresses the importance of emphasis upon potentiality rather than upon norms and single measures of giftedness. It involves movement away from concepts of a single type of giftedness and talent, fixed intelligence and beliefs in predetermined development. In the following chapters, an effort will be made to outline educational goals, identification procedures, strategies of motivation, and methods and materials of instruction appropriate for the education of gifted and talented children in the regular classroom.

NOTE: Since this book was written and type-set, Howard Gardner has proposed additional intelligences in a two-installment article entitled "Are There Additional Intelligences? The Case for Naturalist, Spiritual, and Existential Intelligences," in *Gifted Education Press Quarterly,* Volume 11, Numbers 2 and 3. However, no instructional or assessment material has yet been published, insofar as the authors know.

2

Goals In Teaching Gifted And Talented Children

NEED FOR GOALS

G IFTED AND TALENTED CHILDREN are an awesomely powerful force. They can advance civilization or destroy it. The creative energies of gifted and talented children need to be activated and guided early, or else they will be lost — or prove dangerous. Thus it is important that the classroom teacher ask "What kind of persons do I want the gifted and talented children I teach to become?"

COMMONLY HELD GOALS

Below are five sets of characteristics which best describe five different kinds of gifted or talented children. Which of these individuals would you want your students to become? Try ranking them from most desirable to least desirable in the blanks at the left of the descriptions.

Student 1. Affectionate, considerate of others, courteous, does work on time, industrious, obedient, remembers well, willing to accept judgments of his/her elders, not bashful, does not disturb existing organization or procedures, not talkative.

Student 2. Self-confident, considerate of others, independent in thinking, asking questions about puzzling things, curious and searching, attempting difficult tasks, receptive of ideas of others, willing to take risks, courteous and polite, versatile and well-rounded.

Student 3. Willing to take risks, curious and searching, independent in thinking, courageous in convictions, independent in judgment, self-starting and initiating, sense of humor, asking questions about puzzling things, attempting difficult tasks.

Student 4. Self-satisfied, domineering and controlling, negativistic and resistant, fearful and apprehensive, fault-finding and objecting, critical of others, conforming, obedient and submissive to authority, timid and shy, unsophisticated.

Student 5.   Adventurous and testing the limits, attempting difficult tasks, curious and searching, independent in judgment and thinking, industrious and busy, self-confident, good sense of humor, sincere and earnest, doing work on time.

Actually four of the five sets of descriptions are composites of the ideal personality suggested by different groups of teachers. The characteristics of the first student are those most valued by a sample of Philippine teachers (Torrance, 1965a). In many ways, this student is a sheer delight to have in classes taught by authoritarian methods and in many social and work groups. Students like this are not likely to initiate projects, disagree with authorities, develop new ideas, or behave creatively.

The second student is the composite ideal of a 1995 sample of teachers from thirteen states in the United States. Students having characteristics like these are likely to initiate projects and develop new ideas, but are likely to experience a great deal of discomfort when such characteristics bring them into conflict with others and cause them to neglect some of the fine points of courtesy. They are the victims of a great amount of ambivalence. They are always asking questions and searching for the truth. They often choose tasks that are too difficult for them and take risks.

The third student is the composite of a sample of 29 teachers and researchers who have studied the creative personality, those who make outstanding creative contributions to society. Students who have these characteristics are independent in judgment, as well as independent in their thinking. Furthermore, they are courageous and persistent in carrying out their ideas. They too ask questions about puzzling things and often attempt tasks that are too difficult for them, but they maintain a good sense of humor.

The fourth student embodies the characteristics rated by the 1995 sample of United States teachers as least essential in making a productive creative personality. Such students would be obedient and submissive to authority. They are likely to be timid and shy, yet secretly haughty and self-satisfied, quite critical of others and fault-finding.

The fifth student is the composite ideal of a sample of teachers in Berlin, Germany (Torrance, 1965a). Students having these characteristics are similar to the ideal of the United States teachers. They are somewhat more adventurous and less likely to be victimized by their ambivalence.

All of these results were obtained by using the checklist of characteristics given in Appendix A. All of the data were collected in 1995 except for those for the Philippine and German teachers. These were obtained in the early 1960s. Data were obtained from the United States sample and changes will be discussed later in this chapter.

Teachers were asked to check characteristics that they believed should be encouraged, double check the characteristics they regard as most important and require special encouragement, and strike out characteristics which should be strongly discouraged. By assigning a value of two to double checks, one to single checks, and minus one to strikeouts, an index of desirability-undesirability was obtained for each characteristic. The characteristics were then ranked. The list of characteristics was compiled by the first author (Torrance, 1962a) on the basis of over fifty studies which had compared the personalities of outstanding creative people with people who were similar but who had not achieved a high level of creative production.

When the ratings of the expert judges of persons having outstanding creative achievements are compared with the composite ratings of various cultural groups, it is clear that all of them have some values which support creative achievement and others which are inimical to such achievement. In addition to the United States, the Philippines, and Germany, we also have data from Western Samoa; Malaya, including schools in the Malayan, Chinese, British, and Tamil cultures; India; and Greece. It appears that all of the cultures thus far studied may be unduly punishing the good guesser, the child who is courageous in his/her convictions, the emotionally sensitive individual, the intuitive thinker, the individual who occasionally regresses and plays or acts childlike, the visionary individual, the individual who is not willing to accept something on mere say-so without evidence. On the other hand, all of them may be giving unduly great rewards for being courteous, prompt, obedient, popular and well liked, willing to accept the judgments of authorities, and being versatile, and well-rounded.

We must consider the fact that these values are gradually undergoing changes. This process is reflected in the changes between the responses of United States teachers and expert judges in 1995 and those given in the early 1960s.

SOME IMPLICATIONS OF THE COMPOSITE IDEAL OF UNITED STATES TEACHERS

It has long been the avowed aim of educators in the United States to provide the kinds of education that permits each child to achieve his/her potentialities. Practically, however, both teachers and parents give evidence of being more concerned about having "good children" in the sense of their being easy to manage, well behaved, and adjusted to social norms. It is rare that we are genuinely willing for children to achieve their potentialities. In fact, there is more concern about "appearing to be" than about "being." Achieving one's potentialities inevitably makes children different and being different almost always brings disapproval. Even when children are different in ways which are defined as socially desirable, they may find themselves under pressure. They may study too hard and learn more than they should. They may be too honest, too courageous, too altruistic, or too affectionate as well as too adventurous, too curious, and too determined.

Let us examine briefly some of the implications suggested by each of the ten top rankings of the United States teachers.

1. **Self-confident.** Self-confidence has risen in importance in the estimation of teachers in the United States in recent years. In the early 1960s, it only ranked eleventh and in 1995, it had risen to first place. Apparently this was a function of cultural change in the direction of emphasis upon this quality. The research on creativity has also continued to give evidence of the importance of self-confidence in facilitating creativity. One must be self-confident to be willing to take risks, be independent in thinking and judgment, willing to attempt difficult tasks, to initiate, and the like. Thus self-confidence is the key to unlocking a host of characteristics important in creative achievement.

2. **Consideration of others.** In the early 1960's, United States teachers ranked being considerate of others first. This characteristic is still recognized as one of the most important of the characteristics listed. The great importance attached by teachers certainly explains why they do not prefer highly creative pupils as found in the Getzels-Jackson Study (1962). Studies show that highly creative people frequently appear to be lacking in consideration of others. They may sacrifice their lives working for the good of others. There are times, however, when they become so involved in the problems which concern them that they do not have the time to appear to be polite and show their consideration for others.

Placing consideration of others near the top of our hierarchy of values may, however, reflect an overemphasis on conformity to the thinking of others and could be carried to such an extreme that it could work against the freeing of potentiality. It may also be an indication of a subtle conditioning for dishonesty, and the kind of consideration teachers and parents have in mind may be a shallow, actually dishonest kind of consideration. At any rate, the high placement of consideration of others identifies an area in which creatively gifted children will need guidance. They could become less disturbing and less difficult to parents, teachers and peers by showing greater consideration of others. Yet should they be encouraged to behave dishonestly, since any conditioning to dishonesty will inevitably diminish genuine creativity?

3. **Independent in thinking.** Since almost all studies of creative persons stress the importance of independence in thinking, it is gratifying to note the high value assigned to this characteristic. Genuine

creative accomplishment, however, requires independence not only in thinking, but also in judgment. The creative person must be able to make judgments independently and stick to them, even though others do not agree. In the beginning, any new idea always makes its originator a minority of one. We know only too well that being a minority of one makes a person uncomfortable. Thus independence in judgment takes great courage. It is more important that children be courteous, do their work on time, be energetic and industrious, be obedient, and remember well than that they be courageous in their convictions. This is a deterrent to genuine creativity.

4. **Asking questions about puzzling things.** Encouraging and permitting children to ask questions about things that puzzle them has risen in importance among United States teachers from a tie for 38th place to fourth place. This represents a tremendously important change in education in the United States. Many educators have spoken out about this matter and have devised ideas and materials to assist teachers in education to better train children in asking questions (Millar, 1992; Torrance & Myers, 1970). Asking questions about missing information, gaps in knowledge, things gone wrong, and the like are important elements in the creative problem solving process and in discovery.

5. **Curiosity.** The high place assigned to curiosity by teachers in the United States is encouraging. Curiosity is an important element in the creative personality and in the creative process. Children lacking curiosity may absorb the information they are required to learn and master the skills of reading, arithmetic, and writing but be tremendously limited in achieving their possibilities. They are not likely to be motivated to continue learning for the rest of their lives.

6. **Attempting difficult tasks.** This characteristic has risen from eighteenth place in the early 1960s among United States teachers to sixth place in 1965. This bodes well for the future of creative achievement in the United States. Only with the willingness to attempt difficult tasks can there be progress. Only when individuals go beyond where they have been before does creativity occur. Children must continually be challenged to go beyond where they have been and to achieve new heights.

7. **Receptive to the ideas of others.** Being receptive to the ideas of others and being willing to consider them remains important in the minds of United States teachers. Being willing to accept the ideas of others on mere say so also continues to be discouraged. In fact, this is given importance in the Future Problem Solving Program that will be discussed in a later chapter. Many alternatives should be considered. Unless there is an atmosphere in which all

alternatives are considered, individuals will not be likely to even suggest new alternatives.

8. **Willing to take risks.** In the early 1960s, this characteristic tied for 28th place among United States teachers, another important change. This would indicate that our culture has become more adventurous and more tolerant of risk-taking. This also bodes well for creative achievement in the United States. The risk should be a calculated one, but there has to be a willingness to make the leap.

9. **Courteous, polite.** There are times when the creative children or adults do not appear to be courteous. They may be too honest or too busy to appear to be courteous — if not too busy with their hands, too busy with their minds. Since courtesy is so highly valued in our society, we may have to help creatively gifted children behave more courteously so that they may survive. However, being courteous is not antithetical to the creative personality.

10. **Versatile, well-rounded.** This characteristic has risen in importance from seventeenth place among United States teachers. This may be inimical to creative development and achievement. People can waste enormous amounts of energy in trying to be well-rounded and make themselves miserable and lacking in self-confidence. Many of the world's most creative achievers have been people who were not well-rounded. When we tell parents this, they are greatly relieved because there is so much pressure to make children well-rounded, particularly the gifted. However, many creative persons achieve in a variety of fields.

In examining the list of characteristics most honored by teachers in the United States in 1995, we have seen some influences which are favorable to the development of the potentialities of gifted and talented children. It is interesting to note that five of the characteristics most honored by United States teachers are included in the top ten characteristics in the ratings of a panel of experts of the most essential characteristics of the productive, creative person. These are: willing to take risks, curiosity, independent in thinking, asking questions about puzzling things, and attempting difficult tasks. Missing are: persistent and persevering, courageous in conviction, independent in judgment, self-starting and initiating, and sense of humor. This is very revealing of our culture.

It is somewhat alarming that teachers hold courage in such low esteem. Studies of the creative person have always stressed its importance. Rollo May (1975), in his book, *The Courage to Create,* sees courage as the most essential characteristic. Kobus Neethling (1994), in his book *The Courage to Shake Hands with Tomorrow,* sees courage as essential to adapting to the future. Neethling himself displayed an enormous amount of courage in teaching creative problem solving in the South African government even including cabinet level people, diplomats, and police. This did much to save South Africa from a revolution when it came time to form the new government. He still works with President Nelson Mandela's office and staff.

In his book, Neethling points out that we live in a time of explosive change — very different to any change that we have ever experienced. It takes vision and vision takes courage. It takes courage to make the creative leap to go beyond where we have ever been before. Furthermore, it takes courage to make a commitment to make the journey. He believes that everyone has the capacity to start a revolution of joy and excitement in living, but it takes courage to use this capacity. In another book, Neethling (1993) maintains that creative people can perform miracles — but this too requires courage.

However, this 1995 study presents a much more encouraging result than the results in the early 1960s. At that time, there were only two of the characteristics most honored by United States teachers included among the top ten characteristics as rated by the expert panel. This is encouraging and indicates that the environment has become more favorable to creative development. This fact should give teachers of the gifted and talented special cause for reassessing their values and goals in teaching them.

INTELLECTUAL GOALS

In emphasizing the kinds of persons gifted and talented children may become, there is no intention to de-emphasize intellectual development. In fact, it is the authors' contention that if we cultivate intellectual courage, independence in thinking and judgment, giving oneself completely to tasks, intuitive thinking, persistence, unwillingness to accept things on mere say-so, curiosity, and the like, we will have little worry about intellectual goals. Children will begin acquiring early the motivations and skills for learning throughout their lives. Their lives will be directed toward the development of potential rather than the achievement of behavioral norms, social adjustment, and the like.

Perhaps it would be well at this point to correct the misunderstanding of some teachers that information, memory, and the memory abilities are not important. Having a good memory and being a good thinker are quite compatible. Facts are indeed the food for thinking. Many of the great thinkers of the past were encyclopedic in their knowledge of what was known at the time in which they lived. Aristotle, da Vinci, Newton, and Darwin were noted for the vastness of their knowledge. Today our store of knowledge is much greater and is increasing at an ever increasing rate.

The development of judgment, critical thinking, and decision-making skills is also important. It has been the authors' experience in working with gifted children that many of them are inhibited in producing ideas by

overdeveloped habits of criticism. It would, of course, be unwise to encourage children to produce unusual ideas without developing habits and
skills of testing and evaluating them.

What we should be concerned about is the development of all of the gifted
child's intellectual abilities. Guilford (1961) maintains that the human organism acquires information, retains it, uses it in generating new information, and evaluates information at each of these steps. Thus, while we
should be concerned that gifted children acquire a great deal of information and retain it, we should not be greatly disturbed if they show little
inclination to become walking encyclopedias. Teachers of gifted children
should be concerned about what kind of persons their students are becoming. What kind of thinking do they engage in? How resourceful are
they? Are they learning to give thoughtful explanations of things they see,
hear, and do? Do they consider their ideas important? Do they relate similar
experiences together to draw conclusions? Do they do some thinking for
themselves? Teachers and parents can use these questions as a guide in
helping gifted children develop their potentialities.

CONCLUSION

One way of summarizing this chapter on goals is expressed by the Manifesto that Torrance (1982) wrote to summarize his conclusions to one of
his longitudinal studies of creative achievement. It expresses the goals
and the conflicts the subjects were experiencing in striving to attain them.

1. Don't be afraid to fall in love with something and pursue it with
   intensity.
2. Know, understand, take pride in, practice, develop, exploit, and
   enjoy your greatest strengths.
3. Learn to free yourself from the expectations of others and to walk
   away from the games they impose on you. Free yourself to play
   your own game.
4. Find a great teacher or mentor who will help you.
5. Don't waste energy trying to be well-rounded.
6. Do what you love and can do well.
7. Learn the skills of interdependence.

3

Identifying Gifted
And Talented Children

ACCEPTANCE of the complex concept of giftedness and talent discussed in the first two chapters commits one unalterably to complexities in identifying such children. The procedures, means, and goals of identifying them under this complex concept become clear when the task is seen as one of searching for indicators of unusual potentialities which, if given intelligent guidance and encouragement, can result in outstanding achievements of value to society. In fact such an approach is actually freer of confusion than the many current procedures that seek to establish some single index of giftedness for use in an almost legalistic way of selecting children for special programs, scholarships, and the like. In this and succeeding chapters an effort will be made to show how this approach can serve as a useful and practical guide in helping gifted and talented children achieve their potentialities.

WHY IDENTIFICATION IS IMPORTANT
ARGUMENTS AGAINST IDENTIFICATION

Many people strongly oppose the identification of giftedness and talent in children. Some people believe that identifying children as "gifted" or "talented" is like placing a curse upon them. Others believe that the damage is not to the child who is identified as gifted or talented, but to those who are not so identified. Others argue that it is futile to identify giftedness or talent in children, because giftedness or talent will somehow emerge from of such a person. They argue that gifted people have always met opposition, ridicule, and scorn and that they always will. Thus, no matter how innately gifted or talented they might be, this giftedness and talent are of no social importance unless the person is able to prevail against these forces.

The authors own observations have convinced them that these arguments are false and lead to dangerous consequences. For example, in our longitudinal studies of creatively gifted children, we have seen children in the process of sacrificing needlessly what promised to be great creative talents. It is true that some of them will sacrifice their creativity only for a while and will regain it when they learn better how to cope with coercive pressures. It is apparent, however, that some never regain the creativity they showed so richly in the third grade. Instead they choose the paths of delinquency, mental illness, or at best a life of mediocrity and unrealized possibilities.

This complaint is hardly valid when a multiple intelligence and talent approach is used in the regular classroom. Under such conditions, many of the children will be identified as gifted or talented in something and practically all of them will be above average in something. The goal is to give every child a chance to attain his/her highest potential and the teaching techniques for accomplishing this are described in this book.

CHANGED BEHAVIOR INDUCED BY IDENTIFICATION

In our longitudinal studies, we also have seen dramatic changes take place in the functioning of a child identified as being creatively gifted. During the first year of these longitudinal studies, the first author was told by most fourth-, fifth-, and sixth-grade teachers that they had some pupils who could not take a test of creative thinking because they could not read or write. Usually we tested these children individually and orally. In some cases, they were tested both with group and individual tests. In almost every class, at least one of these "hopeless cases" turned out to be creatively gifted in some way. When this was discussed with the teacher, he/she usually showed curiosity concerning the potential of the pupil, started asking him/her questions that he/she would ordinarily never have dared ask, and giving him/her assignments to test his/her potentiality. Almost always the teacher was amazed that the pupil knew so much, thought so deeply, and could produce such excellent solutions to problems. In some cases such occurrences became turning points in a child's school career.

Whenever a multiple abilities or talent approach has been applied and reported (Reis, M., & Jordan, T., 1993; Schlichter, 1993; Skromme, 1989; Schlichter & Palmer, 1993; Sisk, 1993; Taylor, 1993; Waldrop, 1993), it has been met with enthusiasm on the part of teachers, parents, and children. Skromme, for example, emphasizes the importance of reporting the results of his 7-abilities. He reports that the children react with increased self-confidence, relief and joy, creativity, and goal directedness.

Taylor refers to his approach as the "multiple talent" approach. He has dramatized his approach by what he refers to as "Taylor's Talent Totem

Figure 3.1. Taylor's talent totem poles — 1984 extend version. *(© 1984 Calvin W. Taylor, in "The Simultaneous Double-Curriculum for Developing Human Resources: A Research Based Theory of Education."* Journal for the Education of the Gifted. *Reprinted by permission.)*

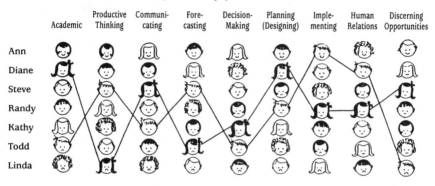

Poles," using the following talents: academic, productive thinking, communicating, forecasting, decision-making, planning (designing), implementing, human relations, and discerning opportunities.

When these identifications are applied, it is found that each individual ranks at different positions on the "totem poles." Again, a majority of them show giftedness on at least one of these talents and almost all of them are above average on at least one of them.

Schlichter and Waldrop call their program "Talents Unlimited." Their "talents" are based on Guilford's Structure of Intellect and Taylor's "Totem Poles," and assessed by the Torrance Tests of Creative Thinking and other indicators. Skromme used the following "abilities" in his "7-Abilities Plan": academic, creativity, dexterity, empathy, judgment, motivation, and personality. Some of what Skromme calls "abilities" are personality and emotional factors, but he tests for them and treats them as abilities that influence success in and out of school.

IDENTIFICATION AS BASIS FOR INDIVIDUALIZING INSTRUCTION

Some teachers and laymen argue that it is useless to identify giftedness and talent because "what is good for the average is good for all." This argument is simply not true. The results of practically every educational experiment that has taken into consideration different levels and kinds of ability provide an argument in favor of the importance of individualized instruction. It is true that in most classrooms the so-called "average" may demand most of the teacher's time and effort. This usually leaves the problem of motivating and guiding the learning and thinking of those who are different from the average.

The authors believe, however, that this condition can be averted with gifted and talented children in the regular classroom. Most of the procedures described in this book involve all children in a classroom and which permit them to respond in terms of their experiences and in terms of their own strengths. Of course, they may also have to rely on mentors, independent learning, and the like to supplement what happens in the classroom. Through cooperative learning, role playing, creative problem solving, creative reading, and the like, everyone learns from one another.

Whether we are concerned about identification of giftedness and talent as a basis for individualizing instruction within a classroom, grouping children for instruction, or acceleration, an effort should be made to consider the kinds of giftedness that make a difference in the way children should be taught. One of the major reasons why the first author had been interested in developing measures of the creative-thinking abilities is that he believes they provide one useful basis in differentiating instruction for different kinds of gifted and talented children. Since abilities and talent at least to some extent constitute a basis of needs and motivations, knowledge about a child's creative-thinking abilities, for example, seems to reveal differential preferences for ways of learning.

A variety of convergent bits of evidence from the research of investigators such as Burkhart (1962), Hutchinson (1961), McConnell (1931), Sisk (1993), and Stolurow (1962) support the conclusion that whenever the way of teaching children is changed, different children become the star learners and thinkers. Similarly, whenever methods of assessing the outcomes of educational experiences are changed, different children emerge as the stars. Stolurow, for example, found that with certain strategies of programming instruction, posttraining achievement is more closely related to measures of originality than to measures of mental age derived from intelligence tests. Hutchinson (1961), by changing regular classroom instruction to give opportunities for different kinds of mental functioning, obtained similar results.

Richert, Alvino, and McDonnel (1982) carried out an extended survey of identification practices and found widespread misuse of instruments. In some cases, instruments were used on inappropriate subpopulations, resulting in cultural bias. In other cases, instruments with inadequate ceilings were used. They made a national report on identification, assessment, and recommendations for comprehensive identification of gifted and talented youth.

Richert (1991) reports that some state and local definitions based on the federal definition inappropriately distinguish between gifted and talented, thus, creating a hierarchy by using the former for general intellectual ability measured primarily by intelligence tests and the latter by the other gifted abilities referred to in the federal definition. These abilities are specific aptitude, creative ability, abilities in the visual and performing arts, and leadership abilities (p. 81). The national report of identification states that measures of academic achievement often screen out the following subpopulations: underachieving, learning disabled, handicapped, and minority students.

De Hahn and Havighurst as early as 1957 listed the following six domains of excellence:

1. **Intellectual ability** encompassing the verbal, number, spatial, memory and reasoning factors of the primary mental abilities.

2. **Creative thinking** including the ability to recognize problems, to be flexible in thinking, to originate ideas or products, or to find new uses for old objects and materials.

3. **Scientific ability** including skills in the use of numbers and algebraic symbols, arithmetic reasoning, curiosity about the natural world, and facility with the scientific method.

4. **Social leadership** is the ability to help a group reach its goals and to improve human relationships within a group.

5. **Mechanical skills** or craft skills depend on manipulative facility, spatial ability, and perception of visual patterns, details, similarities and differences.

6. **Talents in the fine arts** are required of artists, writers, musicians, actors, and dancers.

MOTIVATIONAL EFFECTS OF IDENTIFICATION

Before dismissing the role of identification, a few observations should be made concerning the motivational effects of identification among gifted and talented children. While there is a lack of controlled studies concerning this problem, there is a great deal of evidence indicating that identification and recognition programs can exercise powerful motivating influences on gifted and talented children. An interesting example of such a program is the Bausch & Lomb Honorary Science Awards and Science Scholarships in earlier years. In 1959, Bausch & Lomb made available to the first author a file of letters from award recipients and a copy of the company's follow-up studies. It is clear that many of these gifted young people who later achieved distinguished careers in the sciences would not have considered college education or careers in science, except for this recognition.

Spencer (1957) has reported some interesting outcomes from a state-wide identification project in Oklahoma. As soon as the results of the program were available, the chairman of the Oklahoma Frontiers of Science Foundation sent a letter to the seven thousand bright children identified through the project. One result was that the following fall there was an increase of around 27 per cent in enrollment in science classes in schools that had participated in the program. There was even a 14 per cent increase in enrollment in science and mathematics courses in schools not participating the program. Influences on the individual lives of gifted children were even more touching. One gifted girl in an orphanage showed her letter to an aunt and within a month the aunt and uncle adopted her. This could have been done at any time during the previous several years, but apparently the identification letter produced this major change. The result was that another gifted child received an opportunity to realize her potentialities. Some high-school students who had stopped taking science and mathematics courses resumed them and have since gone on to distinguished careers in college and in their later professional lives.

MOST COMMON PRACTICES IN IDENTIFYING GIFTED CHILDREN

As Gallagher (1964, 1983) pointed out in his book on teaching the gifted child, the means of identifying gifted children during the first two decades of the century was teacher nomination. In many places this is still the sole or chief method. Where nomination is heavily relied upon, teachers often are given various kinds of checklists of characteristics to help them see outstanding potentialities which might otherwise be missed. In most places, however, teacher judgment has been virtually replaced by standard tests of mental ability, usually known as intelligence, or "IQ" tests and standardized achievement tests. One common practice is the use of teacher nomination and scores derived from group intelligence and achievement tests as a means of screening children for more psychological testing. These more intensive testing programs usually include achievement tests, personality tests, an individual intelligence test such as the Stanford-Binet or the Wechsler Intelligence Scale for Children, and interviews. In spite of the many discussions concerning the limitations of intelligence tests, however, most special programs for gifted children about which the authors have been able to obtain data still use rather rigid cutoff points such as IQ's 130, 135, 150, or 160 or achievement at about the 95th percentile.

SOME RECOMMENDED PRACTICES

A number of local, state, and regional agencies have studied problems of identifying gifted children and have formulated recommendations for programs. One such agency is the Southern Regional Education Board through its Project for Education of the Gifted, headed by Virgil Ward (1962). This group found attention being given to the following seven types of data as indicators of giftedness:

1. group intelligence test.
2. teacher judgment.
3. school record, including achievement test scores, and teacher grades.
4. individual intelligence test administered by a qualified person.
5. appraisal of social and emotional maturity and adjustment.
6. parent interviews.
7. pupil ambition and drive.

In its manual on program improvement for the gifted student, Ward's committee recommended that selection should not be based on group intelligence tests alone. They suggested that teacher judgments may be useful, but that teachers have a tendency to recognize as gifted the child who is attractive, well behaved, ambitious, and conforming and fail to see the potentialities of creative children who may be less mannerly, attractive, well behaved, and conforming. In using school records, the Ward group cautioned that poor teacher marks should not be used in excluding a child from programs for gifted children, if the child shows signs of giftedness on the basis of intelligence tests, standardized achievement tests, and the like. They also recommended that individual intelligence tests be used to check on the validity of group intelligence tests. They suggested that parents can supply valuable information for use in identification, especially where young children are concerned. Without making any recommendation, the Ward group pointed out that some successful programs for gifted children have depended upon self-identification. Such programs admit children who wish to try, but they will be dropped or permitted to withdraw if they are unable to maintain the standards of the group.

A number of programs have continued to rely upon teacher identification and have tried to improve the accuracy of the judgments of teachers. The guidance materials supplied by one such group cautions that teachers tend to err in identifying gifted children because they overestimate the intelligence of glib, docile, attractive children, confuse conformity with giftedness, fail to take into account the child's background, and mistake a child who has been coached, pushed, and pressured by parents for a child who is naturally creative and mentally alert. They also caution that some pupils who have potential ability may have failed to develop it for such reasons as: getting off to a poor start in the early grades due to absences, frequent changes in residence, or boring books; concealing ability to avoid being called "a brain" or "an egghead;" various kinds of learning deficits, cultural, physical, or social deprivation.

In the most successful programs for gifted children with which the authors are familiar, those responsible for them have usually decided what kind or kinds of giftedness they want to cultivate, selected students on this basis, and set about trying to develop programs which will capitalize upon the characteristics of giftedness which have been used in the selection process.

SOME OTHER PROPOSALS FOR
IDENTIFYING GIFTEDNESS

With our expanding concept of giftedness and talent and with the development of more effective tests of mental abilities not now adequately sampled in intelligence tests, there now are available instruments that are of more help than those used earlier. If we are concerned about identifying potentialities and developing them, however, we will always have to depend upon something more than test scores. Test data are useful primarily in helping teachers, counselors, and others see possibilities in children that might otherwise be missed; however low performance on certain tests should not blind us to potentialities.

The state of Florida uses information from parents, fellow students, students themselves, media specialists, art education specialists, physical education specialists, music educators, community workers, and school staffs. The forms developed in Hillsborough County for collecting this information are included in Appendix C.

On the basis of emerging knowledge about mental abilities, giftedness and talent, the authors would like to outline several ideas which may be useful in developing ways of identifying gifted and talented children.

1. For some time to come intelligence tests will continue to be useful in identifying and guiding gifted children, but such tests should be supplemented by observations of behavior and by other types of tests such as tests of creative thinking, achievement, and motivation. The traditional lumping together in our thinking of talent, creativity, conformity, and social adjustment has resulted in identification devices saturated with conformity. In many situations outside of the classroom, performance on such devices may actually be negatively related to gifted performance. The requirements of the classroom are often so different from those of the outside world that "the rules of the game seem to have changed." Hoch (1962), Taylor (1964a), and others have pointed out that Terman's gifted subjects (based on IQ) were highly successful in their educational careers, but fewer of them manifested their giftedness through creative contributions.

2. The basis for identifying giftedness and talent should be relevant to the nature of the educational program provided for them. For example, there is much evidence to indicate that the relationship between measures of intelligence and creative ability is so low that identification of gifted children based on measures of intelligence alone misses large

proportions of the creatively gifted. In fact, the first author's data indicate that about 70 per cent of them would be missed. Many special programs for gifted children, however, emphasize independent learning, creative ways of learning, and creative achievement. Creative, independent children would doubtless welcome the special opportunities available in such programs more than would the merely high IQ student and would thrive on such opportunities. On the other hand, it would be quite unfortunate to identify creatively gifted children and offer them educational opportunities which emphasize learning by authority, sticking to the curriculum, doing work on time, purposeless drill, and acceleration.

3. Types of giftedness other than creativeness are likely to be overlooked in classroom situations. Many teachers tend to give credit only for what children are able to write down, especially from the fourth grade onward but sometimes earlier. Even gifted adults differ greatly in their ability to transmit their ideas to writing. Teachers are also likely to overlook certain types of gifted children if they assume that only those children are gifted who engage easily in abstract thinking and therefore respond well to methods of instruction that rely on conceptual and theoretical procedures. This leads to an underestimation of children who are not very enthusiastic about abstract conceptual thinking and yet may be highly responsive and resourceful when given concrete tasks and problems from everyday life. Such children may be able to carry out quite complicated trains of thought, if they are allowed to work in a realistic world. The multiple intelligences concept may change practices, especially if present trends of providing services for gifted and talented children in the regular classroom continue. Lazear (1994) has outlined a plan to assess each of the intelligences identified by Gardner (1983): verbal-linguistic, mathematical, visual-spatial, bodily kinesthetic, musical-rhythmic, interpersonal, and intrapersonal intelligences. These will doubtlessly be refined and new measures developed.

4. Quite obviously giftedness and talent can be identified most effectively when children are placed in situations that require gifted and talented behavior. There have always been a few children who have manifested their giftedness and talent clearly and unmistakenly. Isadora Duncan started teaching her unique form of modern dancing professionally at seven, and at ten, with her mother's permission, gave up school to give full time to her teaching (Goertzel and Goertzel, 1962). While still in elementary school, Fermi designed electric motors which worked, and Vera Brittain wrote novels on scrap paper from her father's pottery factory while she was in elementary school.

Advocates of self-identification have continued to appear. Renzulli and his associates (Renzulli, Reis, & Smith, 1981; Renzulli, 1994) have advocated and successfully experimented with what they have called the Revolving Door Identification Model. Winebrenner (1992) also believes in self-identification and has used a procedure in which students are allowed to complete five or six of the most difficult problems or exercises first, before doing the rest of the assignment. If they successfully meet the criteria established, they are free to use the time they have left over for activities of their own choosing. Both of these procedures combine identification with motivation and allow time for gifted and talented children to spend some time in activities they are in love with.

Although such gifted performances by children are more common than generally assumed, they are not common enough to be of great service in identifying gifted children. A teacher might achieve some of the same advantages, however, by creating classroom situations that call for certain types of gifted and talented performance. Taylor (1964b) has offered a number of very exciting illustrations of how teachers can create such situations to identify creatively gifted children. The following are a few examples:

a. At times let students do most of the planning on their own and make their own decisions and observe which ones are most dependent and which ones have the least need for training and experience in self-guidance.

b. Develop exercises through which children report their inner feelings and impulses and then have them see how well they can intuitively anticipate a correct course of action. (Example: Which is the quickest way to go from school to some remote part of the city, town, or county?) Then check accurately to see whose hunches were best.

c. Pose complex issues and see which children take a hopeful attitude rather than a position that things are in an impossible state of affairs and nothing can be done about them. Creative children stick with difficult and frustrating learning tasks.

d. Have idea-generating sessions to see who comes up with the most ideas, whose ideas bring out the strongest negative reactions from their classmates, and who tends to lead in expressing strong negative reactions. Observe who has the most courage to hold his/her ground or even move ahead, instead of retreating or giving up in the face of negative reactions.

e. Ask students to do a task they have done before, but take away most of the materials and facilities previously available to see who will be the most resourceful in improvising or in accomplishing the task without the usual facilities.

f. Structure some classroom task where those who tolerate uncertainty and ambiguity do better than those who are unable to do so — in other words a situation in which the rewards go to those who keep the problem open and keep working at it with their own resources until they eventually attain a solution.

These are examples of the countless opportunities teachers can create and use in evoking and identifying the kinds of behavior that will reveal glimpses of potentialities. Teachers could not even identify outstanding jumping ability if they depended only upon their observations of how high children just happen to jump in ordinary activities. In order to identify children with outstanding jumping ability, they must create a situation that will motivate and require them to jump.

With the growing acceptance of the multiple intelligences concept in teaching gifted and talented children in the regular classroom, motivation and observation will become more important. With the teaching procedures designed to implement this concept there will be an improvement in skills of observation and identification. Many of these procedures have been described in later chapters.

CONCLUSION

In this chapter we have considered the consequences of the acceptance of a complex concept or giftedness and talent for the process of identification. This task is presented as one of searching for unusual potentialities which, if given sound guidance and encouragement, can result in outstanding achievements of value to society. The importance of identification is discussed and procedures and means of identification are described.

Motivating Gifted And Talented Children To Learn

A LTHOUGH the term *underachiever* seems woefully inappropriate in the light of new insights concerning the measurement of mental abilities and achievement, there is no question but that many gifted and talented children are not motivated to learn and learn little, no matter how their achievement is assessed. Somehow there must be a will to learn.

It is not very helpful to explain the gifted and talented children who are unmotivated to learn by saying that they are "lazy," "indifferent," "uncooperative," "spoiled," or "bad." There are many reasons why teachers should be concerned about such children, even in the early grades. Research indicates (Frankel, 1961; Whitmore, 1980) that once a pattern of "underachievement" has been established, it generally continues and becomes worse. The eventual outcome too frequently is delinquency, school dropout, and mental illness. Whitmore (1980) noted the following characteristics of underachievers: academic anxiety, lowered self-value, defensive authority relations, heightened independence-dependence conflict, interest in social activity, and unrealistic goals.

DEFINITION OF MOTIVATION

Research and theory concerning problems of motivation are so complex that it would be easy to become bogged down just trying to define motivation. Thus the authors have defined motivation very simply as involving all those variables that arouse, sustain, and direct behavior — in our case, the learning of gifted and talented children. This means that gifted students lacking motivation are not sufficiently aroused and sustained to learn at anything near the level of which they are capable.

It is, of course, quite difficult to tell whether a particular child is learning at the level of which he/she is capable, because it is practically impossible to determine what is the potentiality of a child if he/she is not motivated to perform well on the test or other indicators of potential. Yet it is important that teachers give attention to every indicator of potential available to them. Without a knowledge of potential, teachers may place too much pressure on a child who is already too strongly motivated and is unable to learn because of being overanxious, or teachers may be unconcerned about a potentially brilliant student whose achievement is only mediocre.

History is filled with accounts of eminent men and women, unquestionably gifted, who did not achieve very well during certain periods of their school careers. Albert Einstein, Franklin D. Roosevelt, John F. Kennedy, Isadora Duncan, Maria Callas, and Sir Winston Churchill are examples of men and women who at times appeared to be unmotivated to learn what their schools offered and made "C's." Wernher von Braun, the famous space scientist, failed his high-school courses in mathematics and physics. Of course, after he became enthusiastic about rocketry, he excelled in mathematics and physics. Thomas Edison's teacher thought that he was mentally "addled" and his mother withdrew him from school and taught him herself. Edison was motivated to continue to learn throughout his life and contributed numerous inventions even after he was eighty years old.

Actually, it is sometimes difficult to distinguish the gifted or talented child who is not motivated to perform well from average or slow-learning children. This difficulty is beautifully illustrated in some of the experiences of Ronald J. Goldman, when he was an educational psychologist at the University of Reading in England. He and his wife had been operating a youth club for adolescents of average and below average ability. The school records of these youngsters indicated that their IQ's were quite low—around 75 to 90—and that they were very low achievers. Besides this most of them had been engaging in considerable vandalism and hoodlum-type behavior. After working with them in the club for some time and exposing them to a stimulating and responsive environment, Goldman asked them to take an intelligence test and to do as well as they could with it. Apparently they were motivated then to perform in terms of their potential. The results showed that the average IQ of the group was about 25 points higher than their school records showed.

CREATIVE WAYS OF LEARNING AND MOTIVATION

Creative way of learning have a built-in motivation that make unnecessary the application and reapplication of rewards and punishment. If we keep alive the creative processes of students and sensitively guide them, we shall have all of the motivation we need.

Social psychology research has shown that we can usually improve almost any kind of human functioning, increase learning rates, or change undesirable behavior to more desirable behavior by increasing or decreasing motivation in the form of external pressures (rewards or punishments). Most teachers and psychologists think of motivation only in this sense. This may be due either to the fact that this type of motivation is more easily measured and studied than the built-in motivation of creative processes or to the dominance of stimulus-response psychology in professional literature. With unmotivated learners and low achievers, it has been our observation that external pressures, whether in the form of reward or punishment, rarely promote desirable behavior. In fact, we can seldom "make" students learn, behave, study, apply himself, or work harder, if they choose not to do so. With some children and adults, the more we reward them, the worse they behave and the less they learn, and likewise the more we punish them, the worse they behave.

Even when reward and/or punishment succeed temporarily, they do not supply the inner stimulation necessary for continued motivation and achievement. This also seems to be true in much of what is called "behavior modification." Such motivation is short-lived and requires continuous reapplication. The inner stimulation from creative ways of learning makes the reapplication of rewards and punishments unnecessary (Amabile, 1988). Although rewards are less erratic as motivators than punishment, they are still quite erratic in motivating learning. The first author has tried to show that children with school learning problems can be motivated by:

- giving opportunities to use what they learn as tools in their thinking and problem solving;
- giving a chance to communicate what they learn;
- showing an interest in what they have learned rather than in their grades;
- providing learning tasks of appropriate difficulty;
- giving a chance to use their best abilities;
- permitting them to learn in their preferred ways;
- recognizing and acknowledging many different kinds of excellence;
- and giving genuine purpose and meaning to learning experiences.

We shall attempt to show why creative ways of learning have a built-in motivation for achievement and to identify some of the most essential educational methods for facilitating creative ways of learning.

We could explain the motivating power of creative ways of learning by reminding you of the evidence concerning the importance of person's cognitive and aesthetic needs. It is widely acknowledged that we are inquisitive, exploring kinds of beings, who cannot keep our restless minds inactive even when there are no problems to be solved. We seem to be unable to keep from digging into things, turning ideas over in our minds, trying out new combinations, searching for new relationships, and struggling for new insights. These things result from the power of our cognitive needs — our need to know, to find out. The search for beauty is almost as relentless.

A particular individual may not search for beauty in a painting or in a sonata. Maslow (1954) learned from a young athlete that a perfect tackle could be as aesthetic a product as a sonnet and could be approached in the same spirit of creativity and achievement. From a housewife, he learned that a first-rate soup is more aesthetic and represents a higher level of achievement than a second-rate painting. He learned from a social worker that the creation of an organization to help many people was a thing of beauty. From a psychiatrist, he learned of the aesthetic delight in his everyday job of helping people create themselves. From another man, Maslow learned that the construction of an effective business organization could be an aesthetic experience.

Stimulus-response psychology with its motivation by rewards and punishments may actually create obstacles to the genuine kind of motivation that results in continued learning and meaningful learning. There may be conforming behavior, but rarely that "wanting to know" so important in continued learning. The drill common in much stimulus-response learning and adequate reinforcement of desired responses is frequently so monotonous that there is the same effect as we find in fatigue and exhaustion. Many children regard stimulus-response learning as drudgery; there is a lack of intrinsic interest; there is no fun. Frequently stimulus-response learning requires unquestioning acceptance of customs and traditions, conventionality and uncritical imitation of contemporaries, slavery to rules and proverbs, and slavery to details without attention to ability to organize and systematize the information acquired. Frequently, such learning leaves little energy for continued learning. Thus, there is little wonder that reinforcements have to be reapplied continuously in order to keep the processes of learning and achievement going.

WHY UNMOTIVATED GIFTED AND TALENTED CHILDREN ARE SO POORLY MOTIVATED

For the remaining part of this chapter, the authors will identify and elaborate on the reasons why unmotivated gifted and talented children are so poorly motivated and what teachers can do about them.

NO CHANCE TO USE WHAT IS LEARNED

Perhaps the most fundamental cause of low motivation for learning is failure to give students a chance to use what they learn as tools in their thinking. Thus students are unable to see that school learning leads to something worthwhile and are thereby robbed of the most important and powerful reward of learning. This leaves them unmotivated and unexcited about learning. What the authors have in mind is an inner stimulation that is sometimes referred to as "intrinsic motivation."

To many teachers motivation means the application of external pressures to promote some type of desirable behavior. This may be due to the emphasis that has been placed in educational psychology on the stimulus-response approach to teaching. It has been the authors' experience that external pressure rarely promotes desirable behavior in unmotivated learners. In fact we can seldom "make" students learn, behave, study, or apply themselves, if they choose not to do so.

Even if external pressures succeed temporarily, they do not supply the inner stimulation necessary for continued motivated learning. Such motivation is short-lived and requires continuous reapplication. If there is inner stimulation and the more intrinsic kinds of rewards are present, such repetition of rewards and punishments is unnecessary. Although rewards are erratic as motivators, the authors are more concerned about the use of punishment to motivate gifted and talented children than they are about rewards. Many observers of teacher behavior, even in special classes for gifted children, report that they are constantly amazed at the hostile and punitive behavior of teachers in the classroom.

The first author cites an actual case of an unmotivated gifted child who has apparently been victimized by punitive approaches to motivation. The story of this student is best told through excerpts from letters received from the child's mother.

He is now thirteen years old and has had a steadily declining academic record which ended in his being retained in the seventh grade this year. . . . He has a burning *main* interest in electronics and rocks and believe me, his knowledge and interest in these two subjects is great.

His teachers, principals, and counselors have told me a confusing variety of things (confusing to me anyway). They all agree he is very bright, very bored (daydreams in class constantly), and very withdrawn though not rebellious: Two teachers have told me the school has destroyed his desire to learn. One teacher told me the school cannot help him because the only "special cases" they are informed enough to help are the "slow" children. Another teacher said to me: "I'll make him work if I have to break his spirit to do it—and ridiculing and shaming him is the only way with children like him. . . ." Last spring, the school counselor and principal decided that flunking him was the only way to make him "buckle down and work or else. . . ." He can't join the different types of science clubs because he doesn't have a B average—to which the principal urged that he take up football.

So many doors closed! Where is the spirit of educating and cultivating the child's natural desire to learn—some seed of it is always there, to some extent or another!

Now, I will tell you of the boy I know, my son. . . . He is an irresponsible scatterbrain-he just can't harness his brain to such unimportant things as taking out the trash when he's hot on the trail of discovering perpetual motion. He *never* daydreams, *loves* to learn, and is always getting books from the library. He is a hard worker; many times he almost collapses trying to work and experiment late in the night. He has energy enough for ten people. He has an outgoing, bubbling personality and a terrific sense of humor. All this he is at home and in the rest of the world *until* he gets to school.

He speaks of wanting to go to an "electric college" but says he'll probably quit school when he's sixteen.

I feel that he is in a steel box—I think he feels he is too and thinks the only way to be free is to get out by quitting.

How can doors be opened, can you tell me? Can you advise or suggest *anything* that could help?

Please, don't be too busy to care or answer me. I just don't know where else to turn!

Problems such as the one just presented would doubtless be much rarer than they are, if we devoted more effort to motivating learning by providing more experiences in school for doing something with what has been learned. Some of the new curricular materials in mathematics, physics, chemistry, biology and other fields should make it easier for teachers to provide such experiences. Such experiences capitalize upon the disciplined use of curiosity, learning to draw suggestive inferences from minimum data, a habit of searching for relationships and analogies, and honest use of evidence.

INTEREST IN WHAT IS LEARNED
RATHER THAN GRADES

Many gifted children are keenly aware of the shallowness and inadequacies of the grading systems to which they are subjected. They would doubtless be more strongly motivated to learn, if their teachers and parents were more interested in what they are actually learning and achieving rather than how well they do on a particular test. This predicament can, of course, be remedied somewhat by the development of more adequate ways of assessing the outcomes of learning experiences. The addition of tests that require creative problem-solving, decision-making, judgment, new organizations and syntheses of data, and the like will help.

Even discounting the inadequacies of present-day achievement tests, we find some interesting clues in the discrepancies between the teacher grades of some gifted children and their performance on difficult achievement based scholarship tests. Drews (1961ab) identified three types of gifted high-school students: social leaders, studious achievers, and creative intellectuals. Of these, the studious achievers attained the highest teacher grades and the creative intellectuals, the lowest. The creative intellectuals, however, excelled the other two groups on difficult standardized achievement tests, sampling a wide range of content and educational skills. During the usual preparation period just before examinations, the social leaders were studying for the first time those things on which they would be graded, though they read very little in general. The studious achievers were also studying; the creative intellectuals, however, might be reading a book on philosophy or a college textbook, none of which would earn them credit in the teacher's grade book.

Many conversations with parents and teachers of gifted children reveal a startling confusion about actual learning or achievement and the conformity behavior necessary for attaining a passing grade. For example, one third-grade teacher complained that a certain gifted girl was failing. She remarked that she could not understand why the child was failing because she was very bright, very active, and very alert. She further commented that in an arithmetic contest she outdid the best arithmetic students in the class. She was reading books well above her grade level. She could hold the class spellbound with her stories and could set any of her classmates down in a spelling contest. This teacher, with her emphasis on conformity to behavioral norms, could not recognize that this child had perhaps learned more than any of her other pupils.

LEARNING TASKS TOO EASY OR TOO DIFFICULT

If learning tasks are consistently too difficult or too easy, gifted and talented students will be unmotivated and as a result will learn little. Let us examine first the case of a gifted boy whose teachers consistently tried to keep his learning tasks too easy. It was not until Ted entered senior high school that it was discovered that somehow his IQ and his classroom number had been interchanged on his cumulative record during his elementary-school years. Ted's mother and older brother were aware that Ted was being treated as a developmentally delayed child during his junior high-school years. He was always being downgraded or ignored by teachers. He was discouraged from undertaking difficult projects. His junior high-school science teacher told Ted's older brother that Ted had no ability for science and should be discouraged in his science interests. A nearby college physics teacher gave Ted some guidance; however, and this teacher remarked on several occasions that he wished that his science majors knew as much science as Ted knew at the time he was in the seventh and eighth grades. It was also at this time that Ted won first place in his region and in the state science fair for his linear accelerator with which he did biological research.

Ted's story reveals a couple of additional points on the motivation of students who are frequently classified incorrectly as slow learners. Ted received a rather low grade on his first physics examination. He could hardly believe his eyes, however, as he felt that he knew thoroughly the subject matter covered by the examination. Somehow he summoned enough boldness to talk with the teacher about his examination, explaining that his answers were compatible with certain recent experiments reported in college texts and physics journals. The physics teacher, fortunately an honest man, admitted that he did not know about these recent findings, but that he would check up on them and give his answer the next day. This was a fortunate experience for Ted, but the situation in chemistry was different. The chemistry teacher insisted that they stick to the "simple, fundamental things" and would not consider some of the more recent knowledge in chemistry, even though what was being taught was erroneous.

During his junior and senior years in high school, Ted won eight major national and state awards for creative achievements in science and did very well on the College Board Examinations, scoring high in science and mathematics and above average in English. Yet he was still regarded as a slow learner by everyone in school except his physics teacher. At the time one of the major awards was announced, a newspaper reporter asked to interview Ted and his science teachers. The physics teacher was delighted and warmly congratulated Ted. The chemistry teacher's only remark was "This is nice, but think of how many good students knew nothing of the competition."

Yoshio Nozu, who translated Torrance's (1965b) *Gifted Children in the Classroom* into Japanese, relates a somewhat similar case. When Torrance visited him in Japan, he was principal of the high school attached to Shimane University. That year, he was asked to integrate a group of high school-age students who had been classified as "mentally defective" into the school. There was one boy who was extremely interested in physics and wanted to take the high school course in physics with superior students. This boy was allowed to enroll in the course and he led the class. Nozu had him retested and it was found that he had an IQ of 115 instead of a "mentally defective" one.

NO CHANCE TO USE BEST ABILITIES

Alert teachers have long been aware of the fact that when they change their methods of teaching, certain children who had appeared to be slow learners become star learners. They have also observed that when they change the nature of the test used in assessing achievement, such as from a multiple-choice test to one requiring creative applications and decision-making, the star learners and slow learners may change positions in class rankings. With some of the recent developments relative to mental abilities, some of these formerly puzzling phenomena are becoming clarified. Many convergent lines of research make it clear that when we change methods of instruction or the nature of instructional materials, children with different kinds of mental abilities become the star learners and nonlearners. Differences in methods of evaluation or in instructional materials bring out still further differences in achievement.

Hutchinson's classic study (1961) helps us understand this problem. In Hutchinson's experimental condition, the methods of instruction were more nearly geared to the full range of mental abilities (divergent, evaluative, and so forth) found in the normal classroom and not the high IQ students. Classroom observations showed that there was a significantly higher proportion of productive thinking in the experimental classrooms than in the control classrooms. In the control group, there was a significant correlation between mental age and the difference achieved on the subject matter test from the pretest to the posttest. In contrast, there was no correlation between mental age and differences achieved on subject matter tests for the experimental groups. The normal classroom instruction thus seems to have been geared to bring into play the abilities measured by the intelligence test to a greater extent than in the experimental conditions. Gains for the high IQ students were not as great in the experimental groups as in the control groups.

In the experimental groups where the methods were more nearly geared to the full range of abilities and not to the high IQ students, new productive and creative stars emerged and the correlations between achievement and the measures of creative thinking rose. In one of the experimental groups, three of the eight students in the lowest quartile on mental age were the creative and productive stars. Similar findings have been reported by several other investigators (Maker, 1984; Sisk, 1993).

NO CHANCE TO LEARN IN PREFERRED WAYS

Not only are there differences in "best abilities," but there are also differences in preferred ways of learning. Since the first author is frequently misunderstood on this point, a further attempt will be made to clarify the issue. In stressing the need for permitting children to learn in creative ways, the author does not intend to imply that methods involving teaching by authority should be abolished. He maintains, however, that the weight of existing evidence indicates that students fundamentally prefer to learn in creative ways—by exploring, questioning, experimenting, manipulating, testing and modifying ideas, and otherwise searching for the truth. This does not mean that it is always good for students to learn creatively. Although the needs and abilities underlying learning in creative ways are universal enough to make this way of learning valuable for all children, creative learning should not be regarded as the exclusive method of education nor even the exclusive method of education for any one child.

It is also human nature to have anchors in reality, and structure in environment, and to have authorities upon whom we depend. Just as individuals differ in the extent to which they prefer to learn creatively, they also differ in the extent to which they require authorities.

LEARNING LACKING IN PURPOSEFULNESS

Motivation may be low in some gifted children because they are asked to learn things that have little or no purpose for them. Perhaps this is one reason why so many theme-a-week experiments have turned out so poorly. Some students are not motivated to learn for high grades or to avoid failing grades. They need more of a purpose to motivate them to write than "writing to be corrected." There is much more purpose if they are writing to communicate something that they have discovered for themselves. This may be one of the reasons why students who spend most of their time reading and discussing perform as well in theme writing as students who have been subjected to a year of the theme-a-week treatment (Heys, 1962). When students discover something new, they seem to be motivated to tell somebody about it; this fact should be useful to teachers in motivating slow learners.

The motivating power of a purpose is illustrated in the case of Tim reported by Dinkmeyer and Dreikurs (1963, p. 65):

Tim does well in creative work but is apt to be in such a hurry that his writing is messy. For an American history assignment, he wrote a poem about Captain John Smith which was so good that each of the other fifth grade classes wanted a copy. Thrilled by this recognition, Tim made three very neat copies for them.

As Dinkmeyer and Dreikurs commented, writing correctly and neatly took on new significance in that there was real purpose for the readability of his poem. The teacher focused on his asset, his creative work, and seized the opportunity to let him recognize for himself the value of neat work.

McKeachie (1958) identifies two methods open to the teacher in developing motivation for learning, and both are related to purposefulness. One of these involves making learning instrumental for the motives a person already has. Using this approach, we try to show students how our courses will contribute to their goals in life. The second approach involves the development of new motives for learning. The first step is to make learning satisfying, and this always involves beginning with the motives students already have. Thus we have to help unmotivated gifted students see that their learning is really useful to them. By our own enthusiasm for our subject matter, we can also make our students aware of the possibilities of joy in learning. McKeachie also suggests that using a variety of teaching methods is another way of motivating learning.

Although the motivation of gifted and talented children is inescapably a complex problem, there are some very obvious things teachers can do to improve the motivation of such children. They can provide more opportunities for doing something with what is learned, be more concerned about what they are learning, adapt the difficulty of the task to the ability and experience level of the learner, teach in ways that give opportunities for using a variety of mental abilities in acquiring information, recognize and reward a variety of kinds of excellence, including social adjustment and character, and give greater purposefulness to what students are expected to learn.

While these things can be done within the framework of a stimulus-response psychology, the authors believe that they will be more successful in motivating gifted and talented children—arousing, sustaining, and directing their behavior—if carried out within the framework of a responsive environment. This calls for the most alert and sensitive kind of direction and guidance (Ferebee, 1950). It means building an atmosphere of receptive listening relieving the fears of the timid and the overtaught or overstimulated, fending off negative criticism and making the learner aware of what is good, stirring the sluggish and deepening the shallow, making sure that every sincere effort to learn brings enough satisfaction to keep the learner willing to try again, and keeping alive the zest and excitement of learning.

CONCLUSION

The problems of motivating gifted and talented children have been examined. New findings regarding abilities and talents give many clues for motivating gifted and talented children. Such instructional devices as creative problem solving, role playing, cooperative learning, and research activities have a built in motivation. Major reasons for lack of motivation are identified, and tested suggestions for avoiding or overcoming them are given.

5

Curriculum For Gifted And Talented Children

TRADITIONAL PROVISIONS

DISCUSSIONS concerning curriculum provisions for the gifted and talented have for the most part been limited to three possibilities: special classes, acceleration, and enrichment (K. E. Anderson, 1960; Fleigler, 1961; Gallagher, 1960, 1983; Sisk, 1985; Torrance, 1960). In the authors' opinion the theory, research and experience focused on these alternatives have not given and are never likely to yield the kind of guidance needed in educating gifted children. This is especially true if we accept the expanding and emerging concept of giftedness and talent described in the first chapter and the goals discussed in the second chapter. In fact, as we look upon efforts centered around these three alternatives in the perspective of emerging knowledge, the inadequacy and crudeness of such efforts are painfully apparent. Yet the results of these experiences and the research related to them provide us with valuable data for responding constructively to the changing conditions of today.

ABILITY GROUPING

The work with special classes and ability groupings has assumed greater homogeneity than has been warranted. If children are grouped according to any single criterion such as reading ability or mental age (intelligence), the children selected as gifted and talented will still differ in such abilities as mathematical ability, creative thinking abilities, writing ability, and many others. As already mentioned, the first author's research indicates that among children selected for gifted programs on the basis of mental age or achievement, there is little correlation between measures of creative thinking, such as those described in the first chapter, and measures of intelligence and achievement. This research has also shown that if measures of intelligence alone are used in identifying children for special classes, 70 per cent of those who ranked highest on a test of creative or divergent thinking would be missed. Similarly, if selections were made on the basis of performance on the test of creative thinking, we would miss 70 per cent of those who ranked highest on the test of intelligence.

It must be admitted that research on ability grouping, as crude and as undifferentiated as it has been, has generally shown that the academic achievement of gifted students in narrower range ability groupings tends to be somewhat greater than in broader range ability groups (heterogeneous groups). Rather definitive surveys of grouping practices have been provided by K. E. Anderson (1960), Kulik and Kulik (1991), Passow (1958), Shane (1960). Results have not been uniformly favorable, however, and many important goals of educating gifted children have not been considered in these evaluations. The results certainly indicate that ability grouping does not solve automatically the problems of individualizing instruction.

ACCELERATION

Provisions for acceleration have never been very widespread and have been rather generally opposed by both professional educators and laymen. The research results concerning the effects of acceleration are rather generally favorable, as has been revealed by a number of rather definitive surveys (K. E. Anderson, 1960; Gowan, 1958; Reynolds, 1960; and Van Tassel-Baska, 1986). Terman (1954) and Pressey (1954) have long advocated acceleration. Acceleration has taken the form of early entrance to kindergarten or first grade, grade- and junior high-school acceleration, and advanced placement or early admission into college. Successful projects at each of these levels have been reported. Although the evaluation of the outcomes of these projects has taken into consideration such factors as social adjustment as well as academic achievement, none of these programs has been evaluated in terms of broader concepts of intellectual functioning and the other goals discussed in the second chapter. In fact the primary goal of acceleration usually has been to move students along the educational ladder more rapidly or to get them out of an unchallenging and personally damaging situation.

A substantial body of research indicates that various kinds of acceleration produces consistent and positive achievement gains for gifted students (Daurio, 1979; Kulik & Kulik, 1987, 1991; Shore, Cornell, Robinson & Ward, 1991; Stanley, 1979; Stanley & Benbow, 1986). A recent study by Reis, Burns and Renzulli (1992) substantiates the need for accelerated learning. They report that elementary teachers could eliminate between 39-49% of the curriculum in mathematics and 36-54% of the curriculum in language arts without detrimental effects on the achievement of gifted students, since gifted students already demonstrate mastery of the material prior to instruction.

ENRICHMENT

Most generally approved among the three curriculum alternatives has been enrichment. Its advocates, however, have not been able to produce as good research support as have the advocates of special groups and acceleration (Torrance, 1960). In practice the concepts of the enrichment ideal generally have not been well implemented. Many who reject special grouping and acceleration believe that something more than acceleration is needed. Perhaps one of the needs is to differentiate what is enrichment for what type of child and what is enrichment for less able children. Perhaps another need is to provide plenty of opportunities with unlimited possibilities and to challenge the potentialities of different kinds of gifted and talented children.

It is the authors' hypothesis that sound educational opportunities for gifted and talented children can be provided under all three of the alternatives discussed above. The ideas suggested and described in this chapter and the remainder of this book can be adapted for use under each alternative.

THE ACCELERATED ENRICHMENT MODEL IN TEACHING GIFTED AND TALENTED CHILDREN

Once we have committed ourselves to teaching gifted and talented children in the regular classroom, we are bound to the continuous progress enrichment model. With the goals we have set forth in the opening chapter and the identification principles we have described in the third chapter and with the teaching procedures we have suggested in the remainder of this book, the authors think that it is possible to make the enrichment model far more successful than it has been before.

The procedures we have described are aimed at getting total participation and involvement. Multiple intelligences, the whole brain, and creativity are called into play. The incubation model of teaching, cooperative learning, sociodrama or role playing, and problem solving provide vehicles through which this can be achieved.

We recognize, of course, that all of a child's needs may not be met in the classroom and we have described ways to achieve this through mentors, independent study, and the like.

SOME PROMISING CURRICULUM FRONTIERS FOR GIFTED CHILDREN

It seems to the authors that educational practices traditionally have held back gifted children, especially in those areas in which they really excelled, and have tried to coerce them into becoming more versatile and well-rounded by emphasizing the development of their poorest abilities or more severe disabilities. In a speech before the Association of Educators of Gifted Children the first author (Torrance, 1961) described the situation as an effort to "make flying monkeys abandon such antics" and to "make silent lions roar." At that time, the first author suggested that we change our tactics, encouraging the "monkey to fly" and permitting the "silent lion to keep silent," capitalizing upon abilities more important than roaring ability. These suggestions will be summarized in this chapter.

SELF-INITIATED LEARNING

One of the most promising curriculum frontiers for educating gifted children is self-initiated learning. Provisions for self-initiated learning are necessary in implementing the concept of the responsive environment and the children in the first author's longitudinal studies of creative development who are masters at self-learning, usually outside of the curriculum, and they make excellent use of experts of many kinds. One third-grade girl wanted to learn how to knit. Her mother did not know how to knit, so she began going from door to door until she found someone who could knit and was willing to teach her. She mastered the skill quickly and easily. One fourth-grade boy, who as a second grader gave the first author the clearest and most accurate explanation he has ever heard and seen of the principle of the magnifying glass, became interested in high-speed computers. He went to the experts and rapidly became an expert himself on computers.

Teachers hesitate to encourage gifted and talented children to pursue self-initiated learning activities because this makes the curriculum different for each child who initiates a project of his/her own, because such achievements are difficult to evaluate, or because they do not feel competent to give the guidance needed. Self-initiated learning activities can be used successfully in both special grouping and enrichment plans. Such activities are a vital part of the Strengths and Weaknesses Program of the High Achievers Project at Bloomington, Minnesota. They are also a vital part of the teaching repertoire of some of the most effective elementary and secondary teachers known by the authors.

If the acquisition of the motivations and skills to continue learning throughout one's life is regarded as a part of the curriculum, then concern about making the subject matter the same for all children in a class is reduced. Fears about differences in content can also be reduced, if teachers will give gifted and talented children a chance to communicate their self-initiated learning to the entire class. This is important because students who have a strong desire to communicate to others what they find out through self-initiated learning activities and it thereby becomes more meaningful. This requires, of course, that the teacher occasionally permit gifted and talented students for a time to become the teachers of the class. It gives teachers an opportunity to show how excited they can be about learning and that they regard as important the things that their pupils learn through their self-initiated activities. It also becomes the role of the teacher to help the student gain access to the experts needed as "alter teachers." Most teachers would be surprised to discover how willing even the ablest experts are to embrace the opportunity to teach gifted and talented children who want to learn something that they know.

LEARNING ON ONE'S OWN

Another curriculum frontier for gifted and talented children is the provision for them to do things on their own and to learn on their own tasks assigned by the teacher. The first author (Torrance, 1964) has shown that it is possible to encourage children to do a great deal of writing on their own by reproducing a magazine containing their best work. In another study Fritz (1958) found that gifted seventh-grade children in heterogeneous classes in a split-shift school showed more growth in language development, science, and social studies than did equally gifted children under a full-day school. Only in spelling was there significantly less growth among the split-shift students. In still another study (Torrance, 1964a) found that children in a split-shift school engaged in a larger number of creative activities on their own than children under full-day schedules.

There are times when the teacher would be wise to leave most of the planning of an activity to students. Let them plan in advance and make their own decisions.

ACADEMIC DISCIPLINES AS WAYS OF THINKING

Professional associations (Rosenbloom, 1964) have developed curriculum materials that place emphasis upon their fields of specialization as ways of thinking rather than as accumulated bodies of knowledge. These innovations were not limited to gifted children, but represented an exciting development for them and gave rise to new kinds of gifted children. New curriculum materials were developed by the Physical Science Study Committee (PSSC), the School Mathematics Study Group (SMSG), the American Chemical Society's curriculum projects, the University of Illinois Mathematics Project, and the American Institute of Biological Sciences Curriculum Study Group. Great advances have been reported with computers. Kulik, Bangert, and Williams (1983) state that the effects of computer-based teams seem especially clear in studies of disadvantaged and low aptitude students (p. 22).

Learning by discovery and direct observation is a key to the teaching approach being developed in these materials. Children are being taught to become sensitive to problems and to the gaps in their knowledge and to inquire into ways that will yield solutions to problems and fill gaps in their knowledge. They learn to keep records of their observations and use information in solving other problems. They work with raw data and generate and test ideas from these data.

Through these curriculum revisions, children are exposed to mathematics as mathematicians see it, physics as physicists see it, and history as historians see it.

As schools experiment with these new curriculum materials, it becomes apparent that some students who were mediocre achievers become the high achievers and vice versa. When statistical studies were made to evaluate some of the outcomes of the PSSC physics, it was noted that the usual predictors of achievement could no longer be used with much success. Ornstein (1961) has reported some of the results obtained by the Educational Testing Service in their study of their physics materials. He reports that a substantial number of students who had scored only slightly better than average on the School and College Aptitude Test made gradually higher scores on the special physics tests given during the year. Many of these students scored higher than a large number who were at the top on the predictor tests and presumably were specially gifted. One possible explanation is that the students whose high aptitude scores did not correlate with their achievement test scores prefer to learn by authority and are better at remembering facts and formulas than in the intuitive thinking required by the new approach. Different abilities are involved when instructional materials call for creative ways of learning.

THE RESPONSIVE ENVIRONMENT

Another important curriculum frontier which may be of special service to gifted and talented children is being opened up through experiments in creating responsive environments through which children are propelled by their curiosity. This concept of the responsive environment is illustrated in the experimental work of Moore (1961). Through the natural curiosity of children about electric typewriters, Moore demonstrated that preschool children can learn to read, type, and take dictation without being pushed or forced. Here we have skills being learned in creative ways — skills we have assumed can be taught most economically by authority. With computers now in schools, this idea has been pushed far beyond the Moore experiments as they can manipulate words and numbers.

REVISED CONCEPTS OF READINESS

Educators of gifted and talented children, once they cease their "holding back operations," have had to revise many of their concepts of "readiness" and what can be taught at various ages or educational levels. This frontier has already caused much concern, as indicated by the following newspaper headlines which appeared in the early 1960's:

- Caution Urged in Changing Primary into High Schools
- Don't Turn Grade Schools into High Schools, Educators Warn at Parley
- Reading for Kindergarten, Languages Too Soon Attacked.

About readiness, Bruner (1960) writes:

Experience over the past two decades points to the fact that our schools may be wasting precious years by postponing the teaching of many subjects on the grounds that they are too difficult . . . The essential point often overlooked in the planning of curricula . . . (is that) the basic ideas that lie in the heart of all science and mathematics and the basic schemes that give form to life and literature are powerful.

For this purpose Bruner suggested "the spiral curriculum," one that turns back on itself at higher and higher levels of complexity. With gifted children, some aspects of the curriculum can be grasped at higher levers of complexity than has hitherto been thought possible.

It is characteristic of highly creative people that they attempt tasks that are too difficult for them. They have developed the ability to cope with failure and frustration which inevitably results from this tendency. Had they not attempted such tasks, it is quite unlikely that their great ideas would have been born. The teacher of gifted and talented children should at least occasionally confront them with problems that are too difficult to solve and help them develop the skills for coping with such problems. Without such opportunities, children cannot test the limits of their abilities.

SEARCH FOR SELF AND ONE'S UNIQUENESS

Generally people believe that the elementary period is too early for children to start developing their self-concepts, to start searching for their selves. The trouble is that the process is well under way even before the child enters school. Gifted and talented children are quite concerned by this problem and are likely to be confronted with much contradictory information about themselves. A failure to help them develop clear and realistic self-concepts blocks access to important and exciting frontiers. Gifted and talented children need help in accepting themselves because they may even despise an outstanding "gift" or talent, if this giftedness makes them different from their peers. This makes far too many gifted and talented children willing to emasculate themselves and consciously and unconsciously hide or destroy their talents.

OPENING UP THE FRONTIERS

The following chapters will describe some specific ideas for opening up the promising frontiers in curriculum provisions for gifted children. A few general ideas which should pervade all work with gifted and talented children will be sketched quite briefly in the remainder of this chapter.

REWARDING VARIED TALENTS

Educational research has shown repeatedly that people will develop along whatever lines they find rewarding. Thus the need for rewarding a diversity of talents, ways of learning, educational achievements, and the like is obvious.

HELP CHILDREN RECOGNIZE THE VALUE OF THEIR TALENTS

Teachers will be unable to open up curriculum frontiers for gifted children until they can help them value their potentialities and realize what some of their potentialities are. Otherwise even gifted and talented children will continue to devalue their most valuable assets.

DEVELOP CREATIVE ACCEPTANCE OF LIMITATIONS

Inevitably there are limitations, within both the environment and the individual. Both must be accepted, not cynically, but creatively. In an early classical study of the psychology of inventors, Rossman (1931) found that this characteristic differentiates inventors from noninventors. Noninventors see only the defects in their environment. Inventors, however, take a more constructive approach, saying: "This is the way to do it."

STOP EQUATING DIVERGENCY WITH MENTAL ILLNESS AND DELINQUENCY

One of the big barriers to opening up curriculum frontiers is our practice of equating any kind of divergent behavior with mental illness and/or delinquency. In the first author's studies of highly creative children, there are many evidences that their parents and teachers do not understand them.

CHANGE EMPHASIS
ON SEX ROLES

Overemphasis or misplaced emphasis on sex roles is a serious block to the healthy development of many talents, especially creative ones. It has been pointed out frequently that rarely do women become scientific discoverers, inventors, or composers. If they do make discoveries they tend not to be recognized and rewarded. Overemphasis or misplaced emphasis on sex roles, however, exacts heavy tolls on the potentialities of both sexes and creates serious problems of adjustment to highly creative individuals of both sexes. Many areas of experiencing are placed off limits to children and young people because of their sex, thus reducing their awareness and their capacity to respond constructively to changes. Social changes in recent decades have made the emphasis on sex roles less of a problem than it was. These changes are reflected in Showell and Amram's book (1995) *From Indian Corn to Outer Space: Women Invent in America.* This information has not been widely known and acknowledged, however. There are still problems regarding this matter.

Creativity, by its very nature, requires both sensitivity and independence. In our culture, sensitivity is definitely a feminine virtue while independence is a masculine one. Thus, the highly creative boy is likely to appear to be more effeminate than his peers and the highly creative girl to appear more masculine than hers. Roe (1963), Bar on (1957), and Torrance (1963a) have all cited evidence to support this conclusion.

HELP THE DIVERGENT CHILD
BECOME LESS DIFFICULT

In the first author's studies of creatively gifted children it is evident that many of them bring upon themselves many of their own woes. To open to them the curriculum frontiers suggested herein, teachers may have to help them become less difficult without sacrificing their creativity.

Teachers should help gifted and talented children to realize that they are likely to be given more power to realize their potentialities by being considerate of others than if they neglect such behavior. They should be helped to recognize also that outstanding talents may cause others to feel threatened and make them uncomfortable and afraid. In conserving talent, the problem seems to involve characteristics that are essential to creativity and at the same time helping students acquire skills for avoiding or reducing to a tolerable level the pressures against them.

DEVELOP PRIDE IN THE ACHIEVEMENT OF GIFTED AND TALENTED PUPILS

Teachers miss good opportunities for developing pride in the achievement of gifted and talented students. We have done this in a few areas, but not in those having to do with intellectual excellence. Schools have great pride in athletic teams, bands, and the like. Much is now being done to develop pride in a school's scientific talent, especially at the high-school level. Some school systems have organized elementary-school art shows. Much more could be done, however, to give recognition to schools for their development of intellectual and creative talents.

Acceleration also seems to develop motivation and pride. Van Tassell-Baska (1986) reports that advantages of acceleration include: (1) improved motivation and confidence, and scholarship; (2) prevention of lazy mental habits; (3) early completion of professional training; and (4) reduction of the cost of education. This can be accomplished within the regular classroom with some individualization and by using resources outside the classroom. Appendix D identifies and describes some of the devices for doing this.

REDUCE THE ISOLATION OF THE GIFTED CHILD

Much attention has already been given to the problems involved in reducing the isolation of the gifted and talented child. Isolation has been a favorite technique for coping with individuals having almost any kind of divergent characteristic. Several currents of research (Drews, 1961b; Durrell, 1961; Kulik & Kulik, 1982; Torrance & Arsan, 1963) have suggested that various kinds of groupings, both within classes and into classes, may open up exciting curriculum frontiers for gifted and talented children, especially those who are "different."

PROVIDE SPONSORS OR MENTORS FOR GIFTED AND TALENTED PUPILS

Most people who have achieved creative eminence have always had some other individual who plays the role of "sponsor" or "mentor." This patron or mentor is someone who is not a member of the peer group, but possesses prestige or power in the same social system. The mentor does several things for gifted or talented children. Regardless of the mentor's own views, the mentor encourages and supports the talented individuals in expressing and testing their ideas, in thinking through things for themselves. The mentor protects the individual from the counterreactions of peers long enough to permit them to try out some of their ideas. Mentors can keep opportunities open so that originality can occur.

EXPLOIT THE OPPORTUNITIES OF THE MOMENT

The effective teacher always looks for the high teachable moments which are quite like some of the "great moments of scientific discovery." Much discussion has ensued concerning the role of chance in scientific discovery. Certainly many great discoveries have resulted because someone exploited a chance occurrence, an unexpected incident, or the like. As teachers learn to exploit such moments and train their pupils to do so, there is no question but that unpredicted curriculum frontiers for gifted students will emerge.

DEVELOP A SPIRIT OF MISSION

Studies of outstanding men and women in various fields almost always reveal that such people seem to be impelled by some strong feeling of mission or purpose. They believe that what they are doing is tremendously important and are thereby aroused to "all-out" efforts. When learning and thinking is made to be tremendously important and worthwhile, schools will become exciting places and curriculum frontiers will unfold. Even gifted and talented children will achieve more than we thought possible. Unsuspected potentialities will manifest themselves.

CONCLUSIONS

Traditional curriculum practices for the gifted and talented have been evaluated and new alternatives have been suggested. Such promising curriculum frontiers as self-initiated learning, highlighting strengths, learning on one's own, academic disciplines as ways of thinking, providing a responsive environment, revised concepts of readiness, searching for one's uniqueness, helping develop acceptance of limitations, changing emphasis on sex roles, use of mentor relations, and developing a spirit of mission have been examined.

Creative Problem Solving

TECHNIQUES OF CREATIVE THINKING

ONE OF THE FIRST questions teachers often ask is, can creativity be taught? or Is creativity something that you are born with? When our colleague Gary Davis (1992) is asked this question he says "yes" and "yes." No amount of creativity training can make most of us into a Thomas Edison, an Albert Einstein, a Pablo Casals, an Amadeus Mozart, a Pablo Picasso, an Emily Bronte or Mary Cassatt. There is a genetic base to creativity that must be taken into account; however, every student's personal creativeness can be developed and increased. We know that you can teach techniques of creative thinking and that you can help your students be more creative. Some of your students will come to you with special creative talents that need to be further developed so that they can identify their dreams and begin to implement them to help make the world a richer place for all of us.

WHAT IS CREATIVITY?

One helpful way to conceptualize creativity is to think of the three P's: person, process and product, and some educators have added a fourth P, press or the context in which the student lives. Let's look at the creative person first. Most of the characteristics that you see listed defining creative persons were compiled by psychologists at Berkeley, Frank Barron (1990, 1995) and Donald MacKinnon (1986) and from Torrance (1962a, 1979, 1981, 1963b) who has dedicated his professional life to the study of creativity development in children and adults. Yet when you examine lists of characteristics of creativity, it is important that you remember that not all of the characteristics will be noted in all creative people.

Characteristics of Creative People
- Independent
- Self Confident
- Risk-taking
- High energy level
- Enthusiastic
- Spontaneity
- Adventurous
- Curious
- Sense of Humor
- Playful and childlike
- Wide Interests
- Reflective
- Thorough

When you look at this list of characteristics, think of children that you have previously taught that were creative. Amabile (1989) states that a child's creativity in any domain will depend on three things: (1) skill in the domain, (2) creative working and thinking skills, and (3) intrinsic motivation. She reminds us that some elements of creativity are inborn; some depend on learning and experience; and some depend on social environment. Creative students do dare to be different: they always want to add components to lessons, make changes, challenge rules and traditions and usually want to be center stage. In short, creative students are not always easy to have in the classroom; however, they do enrich the class with their ideas when you are able to properly guide and stimulate them.

To help broaden the list of creative characteristics and to make it more user friendly, Torrance (1981) added the following traits to help teachers and parents recognize creativity and to better understand the creative process.
- Likes to work by him/herself.
- Is a What If person.
- Sees relationships.
- Is full of ideas.
- Imaginative, enjoys pretending.
- High verbal, conversational fluency.
- Flexibility of ideas and thoughts.
- Persistent, persevering, unwilling to give up.
- Constructs, builds, rebuilds.
- Copes with several ideas at once.
- Irritated and bored by the routine and obvious.
- Can occupy time without outside stimulation.
- Prefers to dress differently.
- Goes beyond assigned tasks.

- Experiments with familiar objects to see if they will become something other than what they were intended to be.
- Enjoys telling about his/her discoveries or inventions.
- Finds ways of doing things different from standard procedures.
- Is not afraid to try something new.
- Uses all senses in observing.
- Does not mind consequences of appearing different.

Davis (1983) identifies creative abilities including fluency, flexibility, originality, elaboration, sensitivity to problems, problem defining, visualization, imagination, regression, metamorphical thinking, analysis, synthesis, evaluation, transformation, extending boundaries, intuition, predicting outcomes, resisting premature closure, concentration and logical thinking. We will explore these creative abilities in this chapter and suggest examples of how you can accomplish their development in your classroom.

CREATIVE PROCESS

When you examine the creative process, there are stages that become apparent, these include clarifying the problem, working on it and finding a solution.

Torrance (1981) defines the creativity steps as sensing a problem, forming hypotheses, testing the hypothesis, and communicating the results. Dewey (1938) reduced problem solving to two stages, a state of perplexity followed by searching for material to dispose of the difficulty. The Osborn/Parnes Creative Problem Solving model includes five steps fact finding, problem finding, idea finding, solution finding and acceptance finding.

Parnes (1975) in *Aha: Insight into Creative Behavior* further defines the five steps as:

Fact Finding involves listing all the known facts about the problem and securing as much new data about the problem as possible, as soon as possible. In this step, the problem is often viewed as a mess and may well be ill defined.

Problem Finding involves writing or stating the problem and then attempting to identify the sub problems that make up the major problem. This may lead to a restatement or narrowing of the original problem.

Idea Finding is where students generate as many ideas as possible. The goal is to list as many ideas as possible, giving free reign to imagination.

Solution Finding involves choosing the alternatives generated during the idea finding phase with the greatest potential for solving the problem.

This CPS model is a great way for teachers to teach creative problem solving. Fact finding can be stimulated by asking questions like who, what, when, where, why and how. Problem finding can be stimulated by listing, In What Ways Might I? questions on real problems. One question that teachers might ask is, “In what ways might I stimulate creativity in my students?” Idea finding can be accomplished through brainstorming in which judgment is set aside or deferred. The solution finding stage can be helped by the use of a matrix that lists the criteria to be considered in making choices. Acceptance finding involves making an action plan that will be used to implement the solution.

Shallcross (1981) has simplified the creative learning process into five steps: (a) orientation, (b) preparation, (c) ideation, (d) evaluation, and (e) implementation. Orientation is defining the problem or setting a goal, followed by preparation, or pointing toward the factual or data gathering stage. In the ideation state, divergent thinking is used to arrive at many possible tentative solutions. This stage is followed by evaluation in which a weighted criteria matrix can be used to help choose the most possible solutions. The matrix might look like the following:

Figure 6.1. Matrix for evaluating solutions

Criteria →

Ideas							**Total Score**
1.							
2.							
3.							
4.							
5.							
6.							

The numerical weighting would be:

5. Excellent
4. Good — very
3. Good
2. Fair

In implementation, gifted students take action and draw up a plan. Shallcross (1981) lists ten helpful questions to encourage students to prepare their plan's implementation:

1. What has to happen before anything else can?
2. Who else will be involved?
3. Do I need to convince anyone else of my ideas?
4. What strategy for convincing shall I use?
5. What materials do I need to assemble?
6. What rearranging of schedules is necessary?
7. Does anything else have to be sacrificed in order to implement the idea?
8. When is the best time to start?
9. Is the place for it to happen of concern?
10. What is the best order for the various phases of the plan's implementation?

Sid Parnes recommends that teachers help their students become comfortable with the process using it whenever problems arise in the classroom, including social relation problems. In the curriculum, CPS can help students experience real problems, such as: In what ways might we decrease violence in our school?. When students use the five steps on a daily basis, the creative process becomes habitual and automatic. One student told the second author that he hated CPS because now when he has problems, he has to think. This statement was followed by a big smile of complicity.

USES OF CREATIVE PROBLEM SOLVING IN THE CLASSROOM

When teachers make a concerted effort to use creative problem solving with their students, they are amazed at its versatility. Sisk (1985), in *Creative Teaching of the Gifted*, suggests that art ideation be used in art by asking students to respond to simple squiggles as stimulus pictures or by creating class or school logos. In mathematics, students can use criteria selection and evaluation to select viable solutions in Social Studies projects, thus engaging in interdisciplinary work. In Science, students can apply the problem solving process to environmental concerns. In Health, students can apply the problem solving process to combatting pollution. In Music, they can create original music from singular stimuli, such as four notes. In Language Arts, students can watch film or video without sound and write their own original dialogue. Teachers who use problem solving in their classes report that they can create many applications of the creative problem solving process based on their own students interest and curriculum. Amabile (1983) makes a strong distinction between intrinsic and extrinsic motivation and urges teachers to remember that children and adults perform more creatively when the urge to create comes from within rather than from without. For this reason, open ended choice based on interests of students become essential.

DEVELOPING FLUENCY, FLEXIBILITY, ORIGINALITY, AND ELABORATION

One way to stimulate fluency is to ask your students to think of unusual uses of ordinary objects such as ping pong balls, a cup, a paper napkin, a clothes hanger or other familiar objects. A group of third grade students brainstormed the uses of a paper napkin. Some of their ideas include:

- tear it up and make snowflakes
- ball them up and throw them
- float them to do science experiments
- put into big shoes so they will fit
- paint and use as decoration
- use to clean your desk
- piece together for a tablecloth
- cut up and make a mosaic
- burn to get your hands warm
- shred for the gerbil cage
- put behind your glasses so they won't hurt
- hold up and hide behind
- play drop the napkin
- wave to give up
- ball up lots and put them in pillows
- use as book markers
- staple them together for a soft book
- color them and use them for Christmas balls
- put in your purse to make it look full
- feed it to goats
- drop pieces when you are lost
- use them for patterns for quilting squares
- use in boxes to keep things from breaking
- bunch them up in small balls for plugging ears
- ball up and throw in the air for celebration
- make balls for cats to play with.

The students quickly identified twenty-six items which represents their fluency score. Fluency is calculated by adding all of the responses. Their flexibility score was twenty-five as none of the ideas were repeated and you score one point each time the students display flexibility, starting with the second item. Originality can be measured by asking other third graders to list uses of paper napkins and then tally the ideas that no other students have listed. The uniqueness of any of the responses classifies them as original.

Another way to stimulate fluency, flexibility, originality, and elaboration is to ask students to engage in product improvement. Ask your students to create new products. Exercises such as these stimulate your students thinking in creative ways. In your classroom, you can also stimulate these types of creative thinking by asking students to make lists of all the ways they can fight prejudice. Flexibility can be encouraged by asking the students to take on the perspective of a character in their books or in Social Studies you can ask them to take on different points of view of countries or historical figures. Elaboration can be stimulated by having the students write on a given theme, such as, lions who don't have courage or dolphins that hate water.

PROBLEM SENSITIVITY

Torrance (1979) states that problem sensitivity is one of the most important of all the creative abilities. Activities that teachers can use to stimulate sensitivity to problems include having students look at pictures and ask questions that they think the characters would ask or questions about parts of the picture such as, What questions might you ask about the moon or the wolf in the picture? After your students have experienced the above activity, ask them to write stories about the picture. You will be amazed at how much more interesting their stories become.

Defining the problem is greatly enhanced by the use of the simple statement In What Ways Might I . . . This statement opens the question up to many different responses and also invites the student to own the problem by asking what will you do?

VISUALIZATION AND IMAGINATION

One of the wonderful early books used to stimulate visualization was written by the son of the famous movie producer Cecil DeMille. In the book, *Put Your Mother On the Ceiling*, Richard DeMille (1973) poses a variety of visualizations to stimulate actors and actresses to use their imagination. One favorite activity adapted to young children is to have them imagine a bear that is sitting in the corner. In their imagination, they are asked to change hats on the bear and to have it run around the room. This is all done in their imagination or mind's eye.

METAPHORICAL THINKING

One of the best books to stimulate metaphorical thinking is *Sunflowering* by Stanish (1977). Some of the activities suggested by Stanish include completing sentences such as _____ a balloon or dirty as a _____. Students make metaphors for words like oil _____ or run _____. What animal is like a bass fiddle? Why? A hamburger is like a _____ because _____. How is a jar of paste like a school bell? Which is the toughest, a turtle or a big stone? How is an iceberg like a creative idea?

   Metaphorical thinking can be considered at the center of creative thinking. Most creative ideas are in some way stimulated or initiated in metaphoric thought. With metaphorical thinking one makes connections between the present problem and a related situation. It will be helpful for you to take notice of credits for movies, plays or books, as they often indicate what inspired a given book or the incident upon which it was based. Your students will find these activities fascinating as they learn to experience metaphorical thinking in action in the real world. Another important book on metaphorical thinking is Gordon's (1973) *The Metaphorical Way of Thinking and Knowing.* In this book, Gordon applies Synectics to sensitivity, problem solving and learning situations. Synectics is an imaginative exercise designed by Gordon that uses analogies and metaphors to help the problem solver analyze problems and form different points of view. Synectics uses three types of analogy: (1) fantasy, (2) direct and (3) personal. The fantasy solution means anything is allowed and is free from reality or logic. Direct analogy draws upon a similar situation and personal analogy asks the students to place themselves in the role of the problem itself. Cartoons are also excellent examples of metaphorical thinking, especially where the humor is not readily apparent until the metaphor is realized. For example, a baby in a diaper holding a toy mallet poised above a fat spider using Clint Eastwood's famous line, "Go ahead, make my day!"

   Metaphorical thinking is represented in science and invention. For example, the idea for the locks in the Panama Canal came from scientists using a metaphor of a zipper. In problem solving, students can use metaphorical thinking to stimulate ideas by answering such questions as: What else is like this? What does this remind me of? What have others done?

ANALYSIS, SYNTHESIS AND EVALUATION

To stimulate these higher levels of thinking as defined in Bloom's Taxonomy of Cognitive Objectives, you can ask your students to analyze components or parts, look for relationships, make hypotheses, look for patterns in behavior. In Mathematics, Literature or Science they can note cause and effect. In Social Studies and Science they can synthesize parts into plans, make theories or hunches, make generalizations, create designs and evaluate ideas or products for accuracy, value, efficiency or usefulness.

TRANSFORMATION

Transformation creative abilities involve visualization, imagination and creativity. It is the ability to look at one thing and perceive other possibilities. Guilford (1967) defined transformation as conversion of known information into new entities — changes in meaning, significance, use, interpretation, mood, sensory qualities and shape. Students can practice making transformations by looking at visualizations or visual puzzles: The Young Woman/Old Woman, and the Vase/Face puzzles are shown in Figures 6.2 and 6.3.

Figure 6.2. Young Woman/Old Woman

Figure 6.3. What do you see here?

PREDICTING OUTCOMES

Predicting outcomes can be stimulated by asking students What would happen if? In Science and Social Studies, you can stimulate students to think of the various choice points that individuals experienced that might have redirected history. For example, what would have happened in the United States if George Washington had agreed to be the King of the United States? or if Albert Einstein had accepted the invitation to be President of Israel?

RESISTING PREMATURE CLOSURE

Encourage students to go that extra mile. You can begin by asking them to go beyond a good idea to push for even more different and complex ideas. For example, How else might this be done? Does anyone see another way? The major emphasis is to encourage the students to hold their mind open and defer judgment.

LOGICAL THINKING

Most students love logical thinking because they associate it with puzzles. Davis (1983) lists a number of logical problems for students to think about. Some favorite ones are:

- If something is beautiful, it has to be valuable.
- Joe has one sister, but three brothers-in-law.
- An object has color or else it has no color.
- Joe, a strict vegetarian, prefers fish to beef.
- The twins rode into town by themselves, with Chuck in the middle.
- The headlights of the oncoming car blinded its driver, causing him to run off the road.
- Diamonds are more expensive than pearls, therefore pearls are more expensive than rubies.

Students will enjoy thinking of their own logic statements. You can create a logic box in the classroom in which students can place their ideas. At different times during the day, pull out a logic statement to engage the students in spontaneously thinking originally.

Future problem solving (FPS) is a program that teaches students to use the five step creative model to gather information related to general futuristic problems (e.g. underwater colonization or changing family structures). According to Crabbe (1982), FPS raises student awareness of the future teaches communication skills, and how to use an effective creative problem solving model.

Another excellent program designed to involve students in creative thinking is Oddessy of the Mind, formerly Olympics of the Mind. Teams work for months on long term projects, such as designing and building an air craft that performs certain tasks. At weekly meetings, students practice solving short term, on the spot problems and eventually take part in regional, state, national and international competitions.

Still another program which challenges gifted and talented students and at the same time challenges the other children in the regular classroom is the Invent America Program. This program is sponsored by the U. S. Patent Office that grants patents to the most outstanding inventions each year.

Activities such as these are critical in helping creative students develop their inherent creativity and to develop creative abilities of all children. When students work with these activities, they will develop creative attitudes, as well as, the necessary habits and skills of creative thinking.

CONCLUSION

The skills of creative problem solving provide the key to the success of all of the other methods of instruction described in this book. Creative abilities and the steps in the creative problem solving process have also been offered. Several alternative approaches have been described. Some of the pitfalls of using creative problem solving have been identified and described. Finally, some of the national programs and competitions have been given.

7

Creative Problem Solving
And Role Playing

R OLE PLAYING is an ideal vehicle for teaching gifted and talented children in the regular classroom. At its best role playing is a creative problem solving technique. It aims to involve every child in a classroom at a deep level and it involves both hemispheres of the brain. It also involves all of Gardner's seven intelligences and is exceptionally effective in involving the interpersonal and intrapersonal intelligences in solving problems, developing self concepts and self confidence. Role playing is a kind of experiential learning.

In this chapter, the authors will describe the procedures involved in role playing and some production techniques that will make it more powerful. We will describe how all ranges of ability can be reached. More detailed procedures are described by Torrance, Murdock, and Fletcher (1996) in *Creative Problem Solving Through Role Playing*.

ROLE PLAYING AS A CREATIVE PROBLEM SOLVING PROCESS

Role playing is a creative problem process and can be as deliberate and disciplined as any other creative problem solving approach. The general principles of role playing have been formulated by Moreno (1946) and have been refined by Moreno (1952), Moreno and Moreno (1969), Hansen (1948), Klein (1956), Sisk & Rosselli (1987), and others.

Role playing can be conducted in the ordinary classroom or in practically any other physical setting, if the director or teacher creates the proper atmosphere. Some children find it easier to identify with a role if they are furnished with a single, simple stage prop, such as a cap, helmet, shoe, coat, or even superman gear. The director must be imaginative in transforming an ordinary desk and chair into a ship, a jet aircraft or whatever the occasion calls for.

The objective of role playing is to examine a group or social problem through dramatic methods. In the case of futuristic sociodrama, the problem focus is a problem or conflict which is expected to arise out of some trend or predicted future development. Multiple solutions may be proposed, tested, and evaluated. As new insights or breakthroughs in thinking occur, these too can be practiced and evaluated. The planning, selling, and implementing stages of problem-solving can also be practiced and tested. The production techniques facilitate creative breakthroughs and increase the chances that creative solutions will be produced.

A number of things can be done to produce readiness for role playing. Perhaps the most important thing is to set aside at least one period prior to the role playing for a free and open discussion of the problem to be studied. Efforts should be made to generate as much spontaneity as possible in these discussions. This is a part of the process of becoming aware of puzzling situations, gaps in information, conflicts, dilemmas, and the like. The problem selected for solution should be one that the group members have identified as important to all or most of them.

Although not necessary, the use of music, lights, and decorations can do much to set the right mood for role playing.

The steps in the problem-solving process in role playing are quite similar to those formulated by Osborn (1963) and Parnes (1967) for creative problem-solving as described in the preceding chapter.

Step 1:

Defining the Problem. The director, leader, or teacher should explain to the group that they are going to participate in an unrehearsed skit to try to find some ways of solving some problem of concern to all of them. It is a good idea to begin by asking a series of questions to help define the problem and establish the conflict situation. At this point, the director/teacher accepts all responses to get facts, to broaden understanding of the problem, to word the problem more effectively, and asks other questions to stimulate or provoke further thinking about the real problem or conflict. This produces what is referred to as "the fuzzy problem" or "the mess" and leads to the establishment of the conflict situation (statement of the problem).

Step 2:

Establishing a Situation (Conflict). Culling from the responses, the teacher or director describes a conflict situation in objective and understandable terms. No indication is given as to the direction that the resolution should take. As in creative problem-solving, judgment is deferred. The conflict situation is analogous to problem definition in the creative problem-solving model.

Step 3:

Casting Characters. Participation in roles should be voluntary. The director, however, must be alert in observing the audience for the emergence of new roles and giving encouragement to the timid person who really wants to participate and is saying so by means of body language. Rarely should roles be assigned in advance. Several members of the group may play a particular role, each trying a different approach.

Step 4:

Briefing and Warming Up of Actors and Audience. It is usually a good idea to give the actors a few minutes to plan the setting and to agree upon a direction. While the actors are out of the room, the director/ teacher should warm up the observers (the audience) to the possible alternatives. Members of the audience may be asked to try to identify with one or the other of the protagonists or to observe them from a particular point of view. When the actors return to the room, they can be asked to describe the setting and establish more fully their role identities. A brief but relaxed procedure, it warms up both the audience and the actors.

Step 5:

Acting Out the Situation. Acting out the situation may be a matter of seconds or it may last for 10 or 20 minutes. As teachers or leaders gain experience as sociodrama directors, they will be able to use a variety of production techniques for digging deeper into the problem, increasing the number and originality of the alternatives, getting thinking out of a "rut," and getting group members to make bigger mental leaps in finding better solutions. The director/teacher should watch for areas of conflict among group members, but not give clues or hints concerning the desired outcome. If the acting breaks down because a participant becomes speechless, the director may encourage the actor by saying, "Now, what would he do?" or turning to another actor and saying, "What happens now?" If this does not work, it may be necessary or desirable to "cut" the action. The use of the double technique may also be used to cope with such a crisis.

Efforts should be made to maintain a psychologically safe atmosphere and to give freedom to experiment with new ideas, new behavior, new ways of solving problems. It is in this way that participants come to "see and feel" other ways of "behaving" and get away from "more and better of the same" inadequate behavior.

Step 6:

Cutting the Action. The action should be stopped or "cut" whenever the actors fall hopelessly out of role, or block seriously and are unable to continue; whenever the episode comes to a conclusion; or whenever the director/teacher sees the opportunity to stimulate thinking to a higher level of creativity by using a different episode. A description of some of these production techniques will be given later.

Step 7:

Discussing and Analyzing the Situation, the Behavior and the Ideas Produced. There are many approaches for discussing and analyzing what happens in the role playing. Applying the creative problem-solving model, it would seem desirable to formulate some criteria to use in discussing and evaluating alternatives produced by the actors and audience. In any case, this should be a rather controlled or guided type of discussion wherein the director/teacher tries to help the group redefine the problem and/or see the various possible solutions indicated by the action.

Step 8:

Making Plans for Further Testing and/or Implementing Ideas for New Behavior. There are a variety of practices concerning planning for further testing and/or implementation of ideas generated for new and improved behavior resulting from role playing. If there is time or if there are to be subsequent sessions, the new ideas can be tested in a new role playing session, or, plans may be related to applications outside of the role playing sessions. This step is analogous to the selling, planning, and implementing stage in creative problem-solving. For some time, role playing has been a widely used technique for preparing people to sell and/or to implement new solutions. What happens in Step 8 is quite similar to what has happened through this particular use of role playing.

As Stein (1974) indicates, most discussions about role playing, psychodrama, and sociodrama as techniques for stimulating creativity discuss potential usefulness for hypothesis formation. Usefulness at the hypothesis making (solution finding) stage is obvious because playing a role permits a person to go beyond himself/herself and shed some of the inhibitions that stifle the production of alternative solutions. Playing a role gives a person a kind of license to think, say, and do things he/she would not otherwise do. We have found that the role playing format can facilitate all other stages of the creative problem-solving process as well. Children who have internalized and practiced the creative problem-solving process move spontaneously into such stages as developing criteria, evaluation of alternatives, and implementing solutions when engaged in role playing. Shallcross and Sisk (1985) have successfully used role playing, psychodrama and sociodrama in training sessions at the Creative Problem Solving Institute in Buffalo, New York.

ROLE PLAYING PRODUCTION TECHNIQUES

A variety of production techniques have been developed by Moreno (1946, 1969) and his associates. Some of them seem much better than others for engendering and facilitating the production of creative ideas. We shall identify and describe briefly some of these along with a few that the first author has invented.

Direct Presentation Technique (Moreno & Moreno, 1969).

Group members are asked to act out some problem situation, new situation, conflict situation, or the like related to the statement of and/or solution of the problem under study. In using role playing to study the future, for example, problem situations will usually be anticipated future problems of concern to group members.

Soliloquy Technique.

In the soliloquy, the actors share with the audience their normally hidden and suppressed feelings and thoughts. The actor (protagonist) turns to one side and expresses his/her feelings in a voice different from that used in the dialogue. One type of soliloquy may take place immediately after the enactment of a conflict situation. The protagonist may be walking home, driving, riding a bus, trying to study, or just engaging in reverie. In another type of soliloquy, the portrayal of hidden, unverbalized feelings and thoughts are portrayed by side dialogues parallel with other thoughts and actions. It permits the actors to share experiences which they feared to bring to expression or failed to perceive in the direct presentation.

This production technique frequently evokes original ideas which later stand the test of logic. In the terminology of creative problem-solving, incubation is likely to occur both among the actors and the audience. The time out for soliloquy, though brief, gives a chance for the incubation process to operate and new ideas may burst forth and then be applied immediately in the ongoing dramatization.

Double Technique (Toeman, 1948; Moreno & Moreno, 1969).

In this production technique, one of the actors in a conflict situation is supplied with a double who is placed side by side with the actor and interacts with the actor as "himself/herself." The double tries to develop an identity with the actor in conflict. By bringing out the actor's "other self," the double helps the actor achieve a new and higher level of creative functioning. The Actor-Double situation is usually set up following the use of a Direct Presentation after the actor has withdrawn from the conflict. The actor may imagine being alone in the woods, walking along the street or in a park, or sitting at home. This production technique may also be used following the Soliloquy technique to speed up or facilitate the production of alternative solutions.

The whole idea of Double Technique (Toeman, 1948) is rooted in ideas concerning creativity in altered states of consciousness. This idea appears in the mythology of many different cultures. Many highly creative people have reported having doubles. The famous French author, de Maupassant, reported that his double would come into his room and dictate his work to him. In executing the double technique, the protagonist and the double are on the stage together and the double acts as the protagonist's invisible "I," the alter ego with whom he/she talks at times but who exists only within him/herself. This invisible double in role playing is projected into space, embodied by a real person and experienced as outside of the protagonist. The double may try to stir the protagonist to reach deeper levels of consciousness. He/she reaches for those images which a person would reveal when talking to him/herself in privacy. It is a shared task. In one sense, it is dyadic brainstorming at a very intense level. The protagonist may experience many kinds of resistance. The double makes use of this resistance to suggest even more diverse ideas or solutions and to work through to deeper and more expanded states of consciousness.

In using role playing as a deliberate method of solving problems creatively, the director may instruct the double and the protagonist to engage in dyadic brainstorming for alternative solutions. At times, it may even be useful to have someone in the group record the alternatives produced. At the end of the dyadic brainstorming, the audience can be given an opportunity to add alternatives that did not occur on the stage.

Multiple Double Technique (Moreno & Moreno, 1969).

This is a variation of the "standard" double technique and is especially useful for bringing different points of view to bear on a conflict situation and provides a good vehicle for group brainstorming. The actor in the conflict situation is on stage with two or more doubles. Each portrays another part of the actor (different moods, different psychological perspectives, etc.).

The production technique is especially effective when turned into a group brainstorming session, involving from three to six people. The traditional rules of brainstorming may be applied or they may be relaxed. If brainstorming rules (Osborn, 1963) are relaxed and negative criticism occurs, one of the doubles can talk back in a way that is not possible in ordinary brainstorming. This may heighten breakthrough ideas. After such a brainstorming session, additional ideas may be obtained from members of the audience who were identifying with one of the actors.

Identifying Double and Contrary Double Technique (Pankratz & Buchan, 1965).

This technique is a variation of the Multiple Double Technique. The protagonist is given an identifying double and a contrary double to represent the "good" and "bad" parts of his/her thoughts. These two doubles are encouraged by the director to influence the protagonist. The doubles may be quite forceful with their lies, promises, and distortions. The protagonist is encouraged to evaluate carefully both sides of the issue or conflict.

Mirror Technique (Moreno & Moreno, 1969).

In this production technique, another actor represents the original actor in the conflict situation, copying the original actor's behavior patterns and showing him/her "as in a mirror" how other people experience him/her. This technique may help the audience and actors become aware of emotional blocks to conflict resolution.

The Mirror Technique an effective variation of the Double Technique can be produced in role playing when the protagonist leaves a conflict situation involving two or more alter egos. The alter egos can then mimic, as frequently occurs in real life, the behavior of the protagonist. This variation of the Mirror Technique makes it clear to the group that more of the same kind of behavior will only make matters worse and that the problem situation should be restructured and the problem redefined. Once this happens, the group is ready to produce and test solutions quite different from the ones being used.

The Mirror Technique may be used in role playing when the actor cannot represent the role. The mirror may be exaggerated, employing techniques of deliberate distortion in order to arouse the protagonist or a member of the audience to correct what he/she feels is not the accurate enactment and interpretation of the role. In role playing, the audience may become the protagonist and react to two or more mirror presentations of some human drama relevant to the central conflict.

Role Reversal Technique (Moreno & Moreno, 1969).

In this particular technique, two actors in the conflict situation exchange roles—a mother becomes a child and the child becomes the mother; a teacher becomes a pupil and a pupil becomes a teacher. Distortion of the "other" may be brought to the surface, explored, and corrected in action, and new solutions may emerge. In role playing, representatives of different social roles should reverse roles. For example, a black person should play a white person's role and vice verse.

Many teachers have reported that through role reversal, they can get to preconscious thinking within a single one-hour session. By reversing roles one actor tries to identify with another. Experience has shown that persons who are intimately acquainted reverse roles more easily than those who are separated by a wide psychological, ethnic, or cultural distance. In role playing, however, there are values to be derived from errors in identification due to this distance and misunderstandings can at times be reduced.

Future Projection Technique (Yablonsky, 1976).

In using role playing to study the future, this production technique is, of course, quite basic. In it, the actors show how they think the conflict will "shape up" in the future. An intense, effective warm-up is highly essential, and the known particulars and specifics of the situation should be given. Generally, this will involve dyadic brainstorming between the director and the protagonist. However, the audience may also help construct the future situation, pooling their already acquired information about the future. Daydreaming, expanded awareness, internal scanning, and stored memories are the major states of consciousness likely to be tapped by this production technique.

Auxiliary World Technique.

The entire future world of the actor is structured through a series of acts or episodes as he/she envisions them. Each of these acts should portray some part of the actor's future world that is likely to influence the behavior of members of the group and have consequences for the resolution of the conflict situation. Basically, this production technique facilitates daydreaming, internal scanning, and expanded awareness.

Magic Shop Technique (Moreno, 1946).

The Magic Shop Technique is useful in providing groups with insights into their real goals and desires in life. In studying the future, it provides a natural vehicle for testing out and evaluating new alternative life styles. The group or a representative of the group is confronted by the proprietor of the Magic Shop, who may be either another actor or the director. In this confrontation, the proprietor offers the group anything that they may want in the future, such as an end of racial discrimination, elimination of pollution, increased intelligence or creativity, a particular style of life, and the like. The proprietor demands as payment something that the group may also value, such as leisure, a high standard of living. This places the group in a dilemma and usually brings about immediate introspection or internal scanning. The result of this confrontation is an acceptance or rejection of the "bargain" or, as occurs in many cases, the inability of the customer to make a decision. To push thinking further, such techniques as Soliloquy, Double, Multiple Double, etc. may be used to facilitate reflection, meditation, daydreaming, and expanded awareness.

Dream/Fantasy Technique (Z. T. Moreno, 1959).

This production technique allows a group to enact its dreams and hopes and test them. Or the technique may put delusions and fantasies about the future to a test. Once they are produced, they can be tamed or modified.

Sociodramatic Dance Technique (Fine, Daly, & Fine, 1962).

In this production technique participants sit in a circle and listen to music. They become warmed up at their own pace. It can be combined with other production techniques such as double ego, multiple role playing, etc. It is a non-verbal approach that is useful for emotional expression or learning new behavior.

"Silent" Auxiliary Ego Technique (Smith, 1950).

In this production technique, the actors communicate by gesture rather than speech and activities are suggested in the same manner. New ideas and original solutions may emerge.

Magic Net Technique (Torrance, 1970; Torrance & Myers, 1970).

This technique is especially useful for warm-up purposes in heightening anticipation and expectations. About five volunteers are given the "Magic Net" (pieces of nylon net in various colors). Having created an atmosphere of "magic," these volunteers imagine that they have been transported into some future and are asked to name their future roles. The director then gives the group a future problem and the audience is asked to make up a story to solve the problem, using the characters that have been transformed by the magic net. The storyteller (problem-solver) is also supplied with a magic net, distinctly different from those of the role players. As the storyteller relates the story, the actors mime the action. This technique is especially useful with young children, some emotionally disturbed children, and developmentally delayed children.

Reality Level Role Playing.

An entire classroom, school, or other learning situation may be turned into a stage through Reality Level Role Playing. Perhaps the most commonly practiced Reality Level Role Playing has been the application of the Role Reversal technique to real life situations. In the home, the father and the mother may reverse roles or one of the children may exchange roles with one of the parents. In the school, the teacher may take the role of a student and a student may take the role of the teacher. Reality Level Role Playing may be more inclusive, however, and may involve an entire class in establishing a community or some other social group faced with a future problem. A very powerful description of Reality Level Role Playing is found in *A Class Divided* by Peters (1971). For one week the teacher treated as inferior all children with brown eyes and as superior children with blue eyes. Later, the direction of the prejudice was reversed and the brown eyed children became the favored group and the blue eyed children became the disfavored group. Such real-life experiments can be made more powerful by injecting the creative problem-solving process to understand the problems involved, define them, search for solutions, evaluate alternatives, and to test the best alternatives.

Cautions and Guidelines

Since role playing is a very powerful learning medium and involves simultaneously the cognitive, affective, and psychomotor domains, many teachers are reluctant to "try it." Certainly specialized training and supervised practice is desirable. However, most teachers who are otherwise adequately trained and reasonably spontaneous and responsive can master this methodology because it makes use of natural and spontaneous human behaviors. Nevertheless, any teaching methodology can be misused and those who use role playing should be aware of ordinary cautions.

1. ***Keep clear of psychotherapy.*** Remember the differentiation between psychodrama and role playing. There should be a problem-solving orientation. Guide the group away from situations that will result in personal exposures. This can be done by the briefing and keeping the analysis on the *roles of the actors* and not on the persons who play them.

2. ***Remember that your purposes are educational and not entertainment.*** In large classes, some members will want to insist that the actors speak or stand in a certain way to accommodate the audience. The director/teacher must remind them of the purpose of the role playing and help them understand that such insistence may interfere with the group's problem solving processes.

3. ***Do not try to rush role playing.*** Use some other method if there is not enough time. This does not mean that a brief role playing interlude might not be effective in a group discussion, lecture, demonstration or the like. However, there should be adequate time for analysis and discussion. The agenda needs to be flexible and the director/teacher willing to let one thing lead to another even though many decisions have to be made concerning the direction.

4. ***Role playing is an educational methodology and is not an end in itself.*** Information needs to be fed into the process from many sources—from books, informants within the group, interviews with experts, etc. A great deal of fusion of the cognitive, emotional, and psychomotor elements will occurs spontaneously, but some guidance is required from the director/teacher who must keep clearly in mind education goals as well as the goals of particular disciplines. The director/teacher can quickly assess many objectives by observing the nonverbal behavior of the group, obtaining a show of hands, or by brief written responses.

5. *The problem or conflict of the role playing should be one of interest and concern of the participants.* The problems and conflicts should arise jointly from the subject matter of the discipline and the interests and concerns of the particular group of learners.

6. *The role playing should be at the level of understanding and maturity of the group.* A knowledge of developmental psychology is helpful, but if the director/teacher permits members of the group to evolve the problems or conflicts to be studied, the role playing will usually be at the group's level of understanding and maturity.

7. *Such things as racial and ethnic prejudice, sex stereotypes, occupational stereotypes, work values, and the like frequently go deep and do not change easily.* Do not look for quick miracles. Do not push. Behavior will change only so fast.

8. *Role playing is a democratic educational methodology.* It is based on the premise that people can learn to solve problems and can be encouraged to think for themselves. There is an assumption that free people should know the facts, should be critical (not negative but constructive) of their environment, methods, and results, and should know how to change them.

9. *Recognize that role playing is an open-ended methodology and do not attempt to set up role playing so there is only one possible answer to the problem.* Also resist telling the answers yourself.

10. Rarely do actors in role playing lose control of their behavior. *One of its purposes is to help people to learn to manage their behavior more adequately.* Even in healthy groups and expert direction, there will occasionally be some loss of control by an actor. Usually, such incidents can be handled within the context of role playing and used to attain important learning goals. A director/teacher should go ahead and handle them forthrightly and constructively.

    For example, a student of the first author who was a teacher of many years of experience, encountered such an incident in one of the first role playing sessions that she conducted. She was serving as a guest instructor in an undergraduate class in educational psychology. The class wanted to study problems of discipline and began arguing the issues of corporal punishment. The argument was heated and sentiment was quite evenly divided as to whether corporal punishment should ever be used. The director chose for the teacher-role a young woman who had argued most forcefully that no teacher should ever "lay hands" on a child. In the role playing, she was to illustrate alternatives to corporal punishment. Two students were involved, a 9-year old boy and a 9-year old girl. The girl had stolen the boy's "Sugar Daddy" and would not return it. The teacher called upon the principal who came into the classroom and "straightened things out," getting the girl to return the "Sugar Daddy." As soon as the principal had left the room, the boy began running the "Sugar Daddy" through the hair of the girl who had been sucking it. The girl began screaming and the teacher began screaming. The boy would not stop and the teacher suddenly, to her own amazement, slapped the boy very hard. The student in the teacher role was, of course, embarrassed that she had lost control, especially in a matter she felt very strongly about. The leader then encouraged her to soliloquize about her feelings and with the empathy of a double she developed a constructive attitude concerning the incident and the group brainstormed alternative behaviors. It seemed to be a powerful learning experience for the entire class and no one is likely to forget that cognition is not always enough to control affective and psychomotor behavior.

11. **Do not talk too much.** Give students a chance to think and to talk. When you ask a question that requires thought, give time for thought before answering it yourself. Each time you begin talking too quickly, you interrupt the thought processes and problem solving of students.

12. **In role playing, students act out conflicts and problems growing out of the subject matter they are studying.** In the verbally oriented school situation, there is a tendency to just talk about these issues. This does not mean that there should be no verbal discussion in role playing. Role playing is a good device for stimulating group discussion and it gives everyone a common experience and warms them up cognitively, emotionally, and kinesthetically. Yet there will be times when the director/teacher needs to call a halt to the talking and get back to the role playing action.

13. **The warming up process, according to Moreno and Moreno (1969) proceeds from the periphery to the center.** This means that the functioning of participants in role playing is likely to begin on a more superficial level, allowing self-involvement to increase and move them to deeper levels. Thus, problem solving at the beginning of role playing may be rather superficial and logical. However, as warm up proceeds through the use of production techniques such as Soliloquy, Double, and Role Reversal, more creative alternatives are likely to be produced.

14. ***Whenever possible, the principal actor should be permitted to select the time, the place, and the supporting cast.*** The principal actor should be asked to describe the setting to the audience and to the supporting cast in detail.

15. ***Remember that the major goal of every role playing session is to evoke alternative solutions and go beyond what students would be able to do through logic.*** This can usually be attained since both affective and kinesthetic abilities, as well as cognitive ones, are brought into play.

CONCLUSION

Creative problem solving through role playing is a way of involving all the children in the regular classroom at a deep level. This chapter has shown how role playing involves both hemispheres of the brain, all of the modalities and intelligences, especially interpersonal and intrapersonal intelligences. Some of the role playing production techniques for making learning more powerful have been discussed. The steps in the process have been described and discussed. Guidelines for using role playing in classroom learning have been offered.

8

Cooperative Learning

COOPERATIVE LEARNING has been defined as an instructional method, a means of effectively transmitting knowledge and skills to students (Slavin, 1990) and as the instructional use of small groups so that students work together to maximize their own learning and others' learning (Johnson & Johnson, 1991). Cooperative learning models have been used successfully in a variety of classroom settings and several models have been developed by Slavin, at John Hopkins University, TAI, CIRC, STAD and Teams, Games and Tournaments. These will be briefly discussed in this chapter as examples of cooperative learning models.

Team Assisted Individualization (TAI) focuses on mathematics and was devised as a motivational device to provide appropriate skill level material to students below the pre-algebra level. Slavin, Madden and Stevens (1990) wanted TAI to address the classroom problem often faced in individualizing instruction, that of students feeling isolated. In TAI, students are assigned to learning teams of four to five members with a mix of high, average and low achievers.

CIRC is a Cooperative Integrated Reading and Composition model written for reading, writing/language arts and matches pairs of students at different reading levels. Students receive direct instruction from their teachers on a weekly basis, complete independent reading requirements, and work on reading and integrated language arts/writing assignments in cooperative learning groups. Remedial reading students and mainstreamed mentally handicapped students have been included in CIRC learning teams; however, gifted students have not been a focus; yet, they were probably grouped with the high achieving students.

STAD (Student Team-Achievement Division) is a model in which students are divided into four or five member teams. Each team contains high, average and low achievers, boys and girls and representatives of all the racial, ethnic and social groups in a class. The teacher presents new material to the class, and the team members study and practice the material in groups, often working in pairs. At the end of a prescribed lesson, the teacher provides assignments that the students individually complete. Teams, Games, and Tournaments, is somewhat like STAD in that it involves teacher introduction of content, worksheets, team study, individual assignment, team recognition and equal opportunity for success. Yet, STAD is somewhat different in that teacher constructed quizzes are replaced by tournaments between members of different teams.

Another popular cooperative learning model has been developed by Johnson and Johnson (1991). It suggests six member teams comprised of high, average and low ability students. Students are assigned roles including recorder, accuracy coach, summarizer and checker. Teachers introduce content, concepts and strategies and then provide assignments to the cooperative group for completion. In the Johnson and Johnson model, each group produces a single product that is graded for the entire group; however, the students are tested for individual grades. The Johnson and Johnson model is adaptable to most curriculum units, and they recommend that it be used for daily lessons, teaching units, or entire course content. The Johnson and Johnson model has been widely used as a cooperative learning model because of its flexibility and broad applicability to curriculum.

Greenwood, Carta, and Kamps (1990) synthesized the various instructional models in cooperative learning and concluded that four common elements exist:

1. teacher instruction, to introduce new material
2. team practice, to allow students to learn from each other
3. team recognition, to give students opportunities to be winners, thereby relieving motivational problems of low ability students
4. group rewards and cooperative peer relations, to provide students experience in working interdependently and in facilitating mutual friendships.

GOALS AND CHARACTERISTICS OF COOPERATIVE LEARNING:

Primary Goals	Characteristics
Improved student understanding and skill development	Assignments and tasks that require student cooperation in groups
Development of skills of inter-personal cooperation	Group rewards and individual grades
	Structured lessons and student tasks
Positive attitudes toward different individuals and cultures	Peer teaching

Currently many school districts are in the process of modifying their gifted education programs and mandates to include and to emphasize cooperative learning and peer tutoring approaches. However, there are some cautions concerning the use of cooperative learning that need to be addressed.

CAUTIONS CONCERNING
COOPERATIVE LEARNING

Educators of the gifted and talented seldom take issue with the benefits of cooperative learning as a teaching strategy, as reflected in the findings of the comparison study of educators from the middle school movement and gifted education conducted by Gallagher and Coleman (1992). The use of group dynamics or small cooperative learning group approaches have been used with gifted and talented students since the initiation of full time special classes in the Major Work Classes (MWC) program in Cleveland, Ohio, as early as 1925. Also many gifted programs in small districts have employed cluster groups and peer tutoring to provide opportunities for gifted and talented students to advance through regular course curriculum according to their individual abilities. Therefore, it can be safely said that it is not the technique of cooperative learning that is a concern for gifted educators, but the emphasis on the consistent use of mixed ability student groups and the type of curriculum material that the students are asked to complete.

From the authors' personal observations, many gifted students become frustrated in teaching abstract concepts that they understand quite well to fellow students who are neither intellectually ready nor motivated to learn the material. Gifted students report that they enjoy sharing material and concepts with their intellectual peers because through discussion with fellow gifted students, they are able to refine their ideas and add to their personal fund of information.

Another major concern with cooperative learning is that educators may be exploiting the gifted student in an attempt to respond to a current educational trend. As educators seeking to provide an appropriate curriculum for gifted students, we need to remember that such a curriculum is based on needs, interests and abilities of the gifted and talented. When the gifted students' major function in cooperative learning is sharing basic knowledge that they have already mastered or that they can quickly master to other students within a group, this teaching strategy represents a method and curriculum that is appropriate for regular education students, but inappropriate to meet the gifted students' educational needs. Such practices may well be penalizing them academically.

In addition to academic penalties that may be suffered by gifted students in school districts that overuse mixed ability cooperative learning, gifted students may also suffer a loss of personal motivation and begin to experience emotional stress. Gifted students who have spent the greater part of their school day working in heterogeneously grouped settings report that they have become resentful and bored.

GIFTED STUDENT SPEAKS OUT

One gifted student spoke out in the 1993 Winter Issue of the TEMPO, the newsletter for the Texas Association for the Gifted. She said, "Gifted students often end up doing other students' work because of the pressure of the group grade and getting the work done. When this happens, the whole group, even those who did not contribute any work to the project receive a good grade. This is something that has bothered me the last few years of school. It would extremely upset me when I did all of our group work and some of the other students got a good grade for nothing." And most important she says, "The projects offered me no special challenge."

Gifted students want to move ahead, they want to learn all that they can learn, and they do not want to serve only as teachers to other students. Even proponents of cooperative learning recommend that students who already know the material should be accelerated in that subject (Slavin, 1990). Slavin (1991b) further states that individual schools and local districts need to first decide on their curricular goals, and only then identify instructional methods to achieve those goals. Johnson and Johnson (1991) also recommend that high achieving students not always work in cooperative learning groups and that groups not always be heterogeneous.

ROLE OF THE TEACHER IN THE USE OF COOPERATIVE LEARNING

Teachers may require considerable staff development to learn how to meet the individual needs of students in their classrooms and to match student learning to their individual interests and abilities. The ongoing challenge for teachers is how to decide which learning activities are more appropriate for totally heterogeneous groups and which learning activities require that gifted students be able to work in homogeneous cooperative groups with appropriately challenging tasks. In the regular classroom, time is a fixed resource, and when gifted students are organized in cooperative learning groups studying middle level material for the majority of the school day, their opportunity to master advanced material is restricted.

A Nation At Risk (1983) recommended that, ". . . gifted students, may need a curriculum enriched and accelerated beyond even the needs of other students of high ability. We must demand the best effort and performance from all students" (p. 24).

Important factors for teachers to consider are: (1) when to use cooperative learning, and (2) how to appropriately form groups so that students gifted in various ways can share knowledge and ways of knowing and improve their interaction skills in heterogeneous groups, and (3) when to plan activities that require higher level thinking skills in a problem solving situation that will work better with homogeneous groups. If teachers are encouraged to use cooperative learning in a flexible manner, grouping for a specific purpose, cooperative learning can be successfully applied to all students including the gifted and the regular education students. The concept of multiple intelligences enriches the process.

WHAT DOES RESEARCH SAY?

Seven field experiments were conducted by Slavin et al. (1990) that indicate positive effects from the use of TAI with high, average and low achievers. However, none of the seven studies focused on gifted students. Slavin's research concentrates primarily on basic learning skills (Slavin, 1990) and most of the learning taking place in the cooperative learning research studies was conducted on low level processing rather than on high level processing. Because of this, administrators and teachers need to be wary of automatically transferring these research findings to gifted learners. Ellet (1993) further cautions educators that a continuous diet appropriate for the regular education student is inappropriate for gifted students.

Nelson, Gallagher and Coleman (1993) summarize by stating that "Research seems to indicate that cooperative learning can be a useful teaching strategy, but that it is only one among a number of tools necessary to meet the vast ability levels and different varieties of ability in many classrooms. Any curriculum that uses only one single strategy will bore most students and overwhelm others. They recommend that teachers use a variety of strategies to address all children and celebrate their uniqueness rather than hide it or pretend that it doesn't exist." (p. 121)

GUIDELINES FOR FLEXIBLE
USE OF COOPERATIVE LEARNING
IN THE REGULAR CLASSROOM

- Select groups through the use of student birthdays, alphabetically, randomly selecting numbers, numbering off or by student choice. A recommended group size is 4-5 students.

- Initiate cooperative learning by introducing the various roles, and providing badges, hats and the like for easy group recognition. Provide adequate time for the groups to practice the various roles through the use of non threatening material, with the emphasis on learning to use the roles rather than on specific curriculum.

- Use group roles that involve the students such as the checker, reporter, recorder and motivator. Definitions include:
- **Checker** — Gathers materials for the group. Collects homework in the morning and assignments from the group throughout the day.
- **Reporter** — Reports group ideas to the entire class.
- **Recorder** — Writes down group responses.
- **Motivator** — Keeps the group on task. Encourages group and compliments group on their work.
- Creates simple rules to facilitate the use of Cooperative Learning such as the following student generated Manifesto:
  - All students are responsible for the group's behavior.
  - All students need to contribute to the group work.
  - All students need to respect one another in the group and remember that all group members' opinions and ideas are important.
  - Students will ask for teacher assistance when the whole group needs help.

SPECIFIC RECOMMENDATIONS FOR USE OF COOPERATIVE LEARNING WITH GIFTED STUDENTS

Gifted students can profit from working in cooperative groups with students who are two and three years older. From the authors' personal interaction with gifted students, they reveal intense negative feelings of being obliged to spend considerable time in age-peer cooperative learning groups. They report that they don't always "fit in" with their age peers because of widely different interests and their intense yearning to understand things at an advanced and in-depth level. In addition, many gifted and talented students consider themselves poor teachers because of their impatience and sense of perfectionism.

Cooperative learning can be helpful and successful in group investigation because group investigation encourages students to use reference materials, library and media resources and other kinds of information gathering. In group investigation, gifted students can identify their own areas of interest and seek out a variety of opportunities to explore their individual learning needs.

TAI Team Accelerated Instruction with its flexible pacing and its individualized sequences can be combined with cross age grouping to accommodate mathematically gifted students. Cooperative learning groups can also be homogeneously grouped according to achievement, and teachers can provide for gender and ethnicity differentiation in the groups. The key for the use of cooperative learning with gifted students appears to be flexibility.

Kulik (1992) strongly emphasizes flexibility in using cooperative learning with gifted students. He states that if schools in the name of de-tracking eliminate enriched and accelerated classes for their brightest learners, the achievement level of these students will fall dramatically when they are required to do routine work at a routine pace. He states that no one can be certain that there will be a way to repair the harm that will be done if schools eliminate all programs of enrichment and acceleration.

Silverman (1995) further recommends that gifted students be allowed to form their own cooperative learning groups. She states that cooperative learning works best for the gifted when they are able to choose their own groups and to work with other bright, motivated students. Cooperative learning does a strong contribution to life skills such as speaking, listening, arriving at consensus and problem solving. When cooperative learning is used appropriately with gifted and talented students in a regular classroom, it can provide them success, satisfaction and peer esteem. It is important that as educators, we insure that gifted and talented students have the right to be actively learning, processing and producing throughout their school day.

MULTIPLE INTELLIGENCES AND TALENTS

Our new insights about multiple intelligences and talents will enable teachers to make cooperative learning truly effective in teaching gifted and talented children in the regular classroom. Gifted children can be taught many things by fellow students who are not identified as gifted by any of the usual criteria even when multiple criteria are used.

Early in the development of the Future Problem Solving Program, the first author developed some important insights about the problem of group composition. A team from one school had performed better than any other elementary division team on each of the three practice problems. However, the first author and his colleagues were surprised at their poor performance on the Bowl problem. He asked the children what had happened. They said, "Well, we had depended upon Robert for all of our really new ideas, then the rest of us would hitch hike on his ideas and elaborate upon them. About a month before the state Bowl, Robert had moved away. Our teacher replaced him with the smartest boy in the class, but he could not do what Robert had done for us." Robert was highly creative but his intelligence quotient was not high enough to qualify him as "gifted."

Sylvia was considered as stupid (developmentally delayed) through elementary school and she was miserable. As she entered high school, she learned that she had other abilities that enabled her to excel academically. She graduated from a large high school in the upper ten percent of her class. In terms of Gardner's (1994) intelligences, she would probably have ranked low in linguistic and logical-mathematical intelligences, but high in musical, spatial, bodily-kinesthetics, interpersonal, and intrapersonal intelligences. She related her experiences in her high school chemistry class. The students were required to learn the periodic table. To do this, she composed a song about the periodic table by dancing and singing. She made 100% on her memorization of the periodic table and when the first author talked with her ten years later, she could still recite the periodic table. At that time she was an expert mime and made an extremely high right brain score on the first author's Style of Learning and Thinking test. In a regular classroom, a learner of this type could help others use some of the "other intelligences" to learn subject matter.

Seven-year old Margaret had been classified as learning disabled. She had difficulty with spelling, but discovered that she had no difficulty with remembering her spelling words if she sang them. She was so excited that she ran and told her teacher about her discovery. Then she told some of her classmates who were having difficulty with spelling and it worked for them too.

CONCLUSION

In recent years cooperative learning has been found to be a useful instructional device for involving all of the children in a classroom and enriching their learning experiences. Alternative models of cooperative learning have been identified and evaluated. Cautions concerning the use of cooperative learning in the regular classroom have been offered. The different aspects of the teacher's role in using cooperative learning in the regular classroom have been considered. Research concerning cooperative learning has been reviewed briefly. A variety of cooperative methods have been studied and some are more appropriate for gifted and talented students than others.

9

The Incubation Model Of Teaching

THE INCUBATION MODEL of teaching is still another vehicle that is ideally suited to teaching gifted and talented children in the regular classroom. It is ideally suited not only for gifted and talented children but for all of the other children in the regular classroom. All children are curious and want to know. They all anticipate what is coming and their anticipation is heightened when they begin to dig in and begin finding out. This motivates them to incubate about what is learned, to find out more, to ask questions, to experiment, and to use what they have learned.

The authors are not aware of any in depth treatment of incubation. Most authors writing on creativity devote only a paragraph, a page, or at most a few pages about the concept. Many do not discuss the concept at all. Rarely is even a chapter devoted to the topic and we were unable to find a book on the subject. Torrance and Safter (1990) did make a collection of definitions and brief descriptions of incubation. A sample of ten of these definitions are contained in Appendix B. We have selected the ones that give the most information in the simplest form.

THE CONCEPTION AND DEVELOPMENT OF THE INCUBATION MODEL OF TEACHING

More than three decades ago, the first author conceived and began developing this three-stage model. He had been asked by an elementary education textbook publisher to serve as creativity consultant to editors, authors, printers, and artists of their reading and social studies programs. It was his job to prepare guidelines for the staff to aid them in developing their textbooks and other instructional materials.

Two kinds of information seemed essential: information about the hierarchy of creative skills that could be expected at various educational levels so that they would be aware of the kinds of thinking skills that could be expected at various educational levels, and the kinds of learning and thinking activities that might facilitate creative thinking before, during, and after a lesson.

This three-stage model seemed to be a natural way of bringing into play the creative thinking abilities. Before creative thinking can occur, something has to be done to heighten anticipation and expectation and to prepare learners to see clear connections between what they are expected to learn and their future life (the next minute or hour, the next day, the next year, or 25 years from now). After this arousal, it is necessary to help students dig into the problem, acquire more information, encounter the unexpected, and continue deepening expectations. Finally, there must be practice in doing something with the new information, immediately or later.

The creative process embodies the tension or anticipation or expectation, variously described as the warming-up process, rising to the challenge, or attraction to the unknown or puzzling. Arousal of anticipation involves the elicitation of reactions to the information to be presented (in whatever manner) before, during and after the presentation of the information. A major problem is to use this arousal to help students see fundamental relationships among the facts, ideas, and events that constitute the lesson and their past experiences, present problems, and images of the future.

Any skill must be practiced to be developed and perfected, and this applies to thinking skills as well. Thinking is a skill just like playing tennis, driving an automobile, playing the piano, dancing, or bricklaying. Throughout our work with teachers in helping them to teach for creative thinking, we have always been interested to note their surprise when they discover that some students who had hitherto seemed to be slow learners suddenly showed remarkable achievement. Edward de Bono (1985) has made a similar observation in connection with his work with teachers in England and other countries throughout the world. He has reported that many of the teachers involved in teaching the CORT Thinking lessons that he developed have been surprised to find that some students who had previously seemed to be quite dull suddenly turned out to be quite effective thinkers. De Bono commented that these students surprise the teacher, their peers, and sometimes even themselves. He believes that this observation fits the experience that children who do well academically do not necessarily continue to do well in later life when thinking is required for success.

STAGE 1: HEIGHTENING ANTICIPATION

The fundamental purpose of the first stage of the model of instruction that Torrance proposed is to heighten anticipation and expectations and

Figure 9.1. The Incubation Model of Teaching

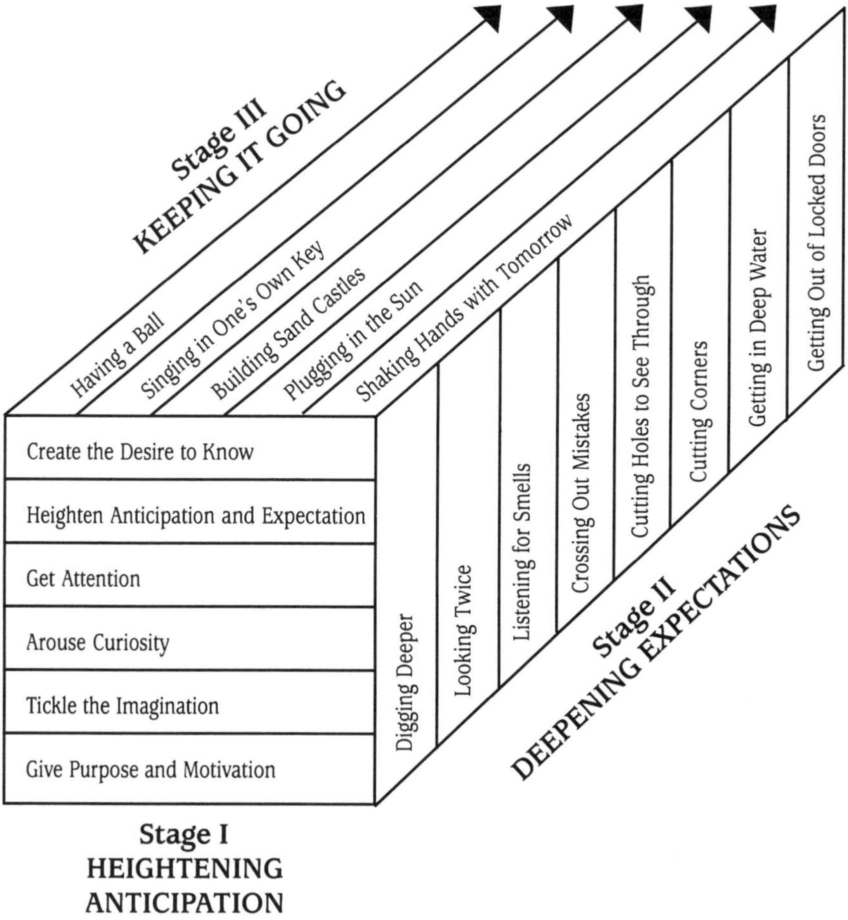

to prepare the learners to make clear connections between what they are expected to learn and something meaningful in their lives.

Essential to any creative behavior is the warm-up process. Warm-up is highly dependent upon the kind and degree of the novelty to be met. Consequently, whatever is done to heighten anticipation before presenting information should facilitate the warm-up process. This encourages creative behavior in responding to the information to be presented.

Generally, the importance of warm-up in classroom learning has been neglected. It has been interesting to note the great importance that has been given to this stage of the creative teaching process by Suggestive-Accelerative Learning and Teaching and the methods of Georgi Lazanov (1978). These methodologies rely upon relaxation and breathing exercises, music, and mind-calming exercises. Role-playing is used in later stages for somewhat different purposes. Torrance (1970) has developed a list of learning activities which he believes will achieve much the same purpose as Moreno's warm-up techniques and those of Lazanov and his adherents. Each of them has been described and illustrated in considerable detail in other sources (Torrance, 1970, 1979). The following will communicate something of the nature of the activities required for implementing the first stage of the proposed model:

1. Confronting ambiguities and uncertainties.

2. Questioning to heighten expectation and anticipation.

3. Creating awareness of a problem to be solved, a possible future need, or a difficulty to be faced.

4. Building on the learners' existing knowledge.

5. Heightening concern about a problem or future need.

6. Stimulating curiosity and desire to know.

7. Making the strange familiar or the familiar strange.

8. Freeing from inhibiting mind sets.

9. Looking at the same information from different viewpoints.

10. Provocative questioning to make the student think of information in new ways.

11. Predicting from limited information.

12. Purposefulness of the lesson made clear, showing the connection between the expected learning and present problems or future career.

13. Only enough structure to give clues and direction.

14. Taking the next step beyond what is known.

15. Physical or bodily warm-up to the information to be presented.

In using activities of the kind listed above, the teacher must keep in mind the purpose of such experiences. In essence, they are:

— to create the desire to know
— to heighten anticipation and expectation
— to get attention
— to arouse curiosity
— to tickle the imagination
— to give purpose and motivation.

STAGE 2:
ENCOUNTERING THE EXPECTED AND UNEXPECTED, AND DEEPENING EXPECTATIONS

For creative thinking, it is not enough to heighten anticipation. Warm-up is necessary, but it is not enough! The surprise of the unanticipated must be encountered! New information must be assimilated. Otherwise, previously learned responses are inadequate and creative thinking is not required. As the lesson unfolds, the heightened anticipation must find fulfillment. The warm-up must be sustained. Heightened anticipation must turn into deepened expectations. It has been found that several different patterns of processing information facilitate this stage. There are no accepted names for them, so we shall use analogies that seem appropriate to us.

The first information processing pattern is called *digging deeper*. Edward de Bono (1973) uses a seemingly somewhat similar analogy to describe vertical thinking. He has likened vertical thinking to digging a hole deeper. The pattern of information processing that we have in mind may dig several holes and may dig some of them deeper. Essentially, however, through the process an effort is made to get beyond the surface or cover and to find out what is glossed over or hidden. The mind diagnoses difficulties, integrates the information available, checks information against hunches, synthesizes diverse kinds of information, elaborates, and diverges.

We like to think of a second pattern of information processing as *looking twice*. To really look twice at information, a person must defer judgment following the first look and keep open to new information and insights. There is a search for more information. Information is evaluated and re-evaluated. Children do this naturally and spontaneously. Frequently, they ask that a book be read a second or third time. For the first reading, they seem to go through the book speedily. During the second and/or third readings, they want to pause and ask questions, make new associations, or make personal association. To practice this pattern of processing information with graduate students, Torrance uses a brief poem. He reads it first, having them simply listen. Then, he asks them to try to visualize what the poem describes. Next, he requests they move their fingers to interpret what is described. Finally, he asks them to move creatively to what is described. We never cease to be amazed at the deepened understandings of the poem that result.

A third pattern of processing is termed *listening for smells*. Sometimes we feel that we do not really know something unless we have a feeling of congruence between two kinds of experiences. This information strategy may make use of any or all of the senses — moving, visualizing, imagining sounds, making sounds, smelling, and feeling textures.

A fourth pattern of information processing that is useful during this second stage is the *listening/talking to a cat* or *crossing out mistakes*. In this strategy, the learner must let the information presented "talk to him/her" and he/she must "talk to the information." In other words, there is a need for developing skills of reading one's own feelings in response to the information encountered. Mistakes will be made in "listening/talking with a cat" and in reading one's feedback about the information encountered, so there must be freedom to "cross out mistakes." Thus, this pattern of information processing involves making guesses, checking, correcting, modifying, re-examining, discarding unpromising facts or solutions, refining, and making the best solutions better.

A fifth information processing strategy is like *cutting holes to see through*. This is accomplished through summarizing, getting the essence, simplifying, and discarding useless and erroneous information. This strategy is especially useful in targeting the problem to be considered or the solution to be implemented. There is always a problem of directing or focusing attention on the specific information that is to be the subject of the thinking.

A sixth information processing strategy is like *cutting corners*. This is done by avoiding useless and irrelevant information and making mental leaps to new insights, "solutions to the mystery or puzzle." This information processing strategy is perhaps most useful in making the best solution better, deciding on the statement of the problem, or in determining a plan of implementation.

A seventh information processing strategy is like *getting in deep water*. This involves searching for unanswered questions, dealing with taboo topics, confronting the unimaginable, being overwhelmed by complexity, or becoming so deeply absorbed as to be unaware of surrounding events.

An eighth and similar information processing strategy is like *getting out of locked doors*. This involves solving the unsolvable, going beyond those "more and better of the same" solutions that make matters worse, and opening up new vistas, new worlds.

The following is a list of some of the kinds of learning activities that Torrance (1970) has suggested for bringing about the kinds of information processing described above:

1. Heightening awareness of problems and difficulties.
2. Accepting limitations constructively as a challenge rather than cynically, improvising with what is available.
3. Encouraging creative personality characteristics or predispositions.
4. Practicing the creative problem solving process in a disciplined systematic manner in dealing with the problem and information at hand.
5. Deliberately and systematically elaborating upon the information presented.

6. Presenting information as incomplete and having learners ask questions to fill gaps.

7. Juxtaposing apparently irrelevant elements.

8. Exploring and examining mysteries and trying to solve them.

9. Preserving open-endedness.

10. Making outcomes not completely predictable.

11. Predicting from limited information.

12. Searching for honesty and realism.

13. Identifying and encouraging the acquisition of new skills for finding out information.

14. Heightening and deliberately using surprises.

15. Encouraging visualization.

STAGE 3: GOING BEYOND AND "KEEPING IT GOING"

For creative thinking to occur and to continue to occur, there must be ample opportunity for one thing to lead to another and to do something with the information encountered. Therefore, it is inevitable that any genuine encouragement of creative thinking must take students beyond the classroom, textbook, and the teacher. Ideas stimulated in a science class or any other part of the curriculum might motivate a student to consult other people, to delve into other kinds of literature or sources of information, to get out into the community, to conduct an original experiment, to write an essay or a poem, to paint an original picture, to solve a problem, or to engage in almost any other kind of investigative or creative behavior.

As in the case of the second stage, there are several information processing strategies that we think are particularly useful in accomplishing the objectives of this third phase of the model, e.g., going beyond the lesson and keeping the learning and thinking processes working on the information presented.

The first of these information processing strategies is like *having a ball*. Schools and colleges, in our opinion, give too little attention to the fun uses of the mind — humor, laughter, and fantasy. This strategy can also be used in the second stage to deepen expectations, but it is probably even more useful in getting students to go beyond the textbook and to keep learning and thinking processes functioning. It is interesting to note that this information strategy is an established part of the Lozanov method as the final phase of a lesson. The final phase consists of educational games to activate the materials learned during the earlier phases.

A second information processing strategy is like *singing in one's own key*. This involves giving the information personal meaning, relating personal experiences to the information, making associations to the information, seeing implications of the information for present problems or future career roles, and using it to solve personal problems.

A third information processing strategy that facilitates the goals of the third stage of the model is like *building sand castles*. It consists of using the information as the basis for imagining, fantasizing, searching for ideal solutions, or otherwise "taking off" from what is read, heard, or encountered.

A fourth information processing strategy that is especially useful in the third stage is like *plugging in the sun*. This may be interpreted either as "hard work" or as "plugging into" available sources of energy or inspiration. Creative thinking does take expensive energy, but it may also be self-renewing and invigorating. This energy source may be new library resources, people resources, place resources, or spiritual resources.

A final information processing strategy is like *shaking hands with tomorrow*. It consists of relating the information to one's projected future career; using the information to enlarge, enrich, and make more accurate the students' images of the future; storing alternative solutions for possible future use; or using the information to propose a solution of a future problem.

The following is a list of some of the kinds of learning activities that seem to facilitate the achievement of the goals of the third stage of the model presented here:

1. Playing with ambiguities.
2. Deepening awareness of a problem, difficulty, or gaps in information.
3. Acknowledging a student's unique potentiality.
4. Heightening concern about a problem.
5. Challenging a constructive response or solution.
6. Seeing a clear relationship between the new information and future careers.
7. Accepting limitations creatively and constructively.
8. Digging still more deeply, going beneath the obvious and accepted.
9. Making divergent thinking legitimate.
10. Elaborating the information given.

11. Encouraging elegant solution, the solution of collision conflicts, unsolved mysteries.

12. Requiring experimentation.

13. Making the familiar strange or the strange familiar.

14. Examining fantasies to find solutions of real problems.

15. Encouraging future projections.

16. Entertaining improbabilities.

17. Creating humor and seeing the humorous in the information presented.

18. Encouraging deferred judgment and the use of some disciplined procedures of problem solving.

19. Relating information to information in another discipline.

20. Looking at the same information in different ways.

21. Encouraging the manipulation of ideas and/or objects.

22. Encouraging multiple hypotheses.

23. Confronting and examining paradoxes.

Others have developed models and procedures which use many of the elements of the incubation model. For example, Frank Williams (1972), used many of them in his *A Total Creativity Program for Individualizing and Humanizing the Learning Process.* He recommended asking provocative questions and described them as "inquiry to bring forth meaning; inquiry to incite knowledge exploration; summons to discover new knowledge" (p. 95). Williams stressed thinking processes (fluency, flexibility, originality, and elaboration) and feeling processes (curiosity, risk taking, complexity, and imagination).

EVALUATION

This model, known as the Incubation Model, was used in the creativity strand of both the Ginn 360 and 720 Reading Programs (Clymer et al., 1969, 1976) and has been applied in all subject matter areas by our students and some of their students. Thus far, all of them have reported excitement, fun, and successful learning experiences. All of them have seemed to be able to apply the model effectively at all level from preschool throughout graduate school and professional schools in all subject matter areas. All have reported results somewhat like those of Plooster (1972) following the field testing of Reading 360:

These are only a few of the many activities that the Reading 360 Program initiated for first graders. The children became very enthusiastic about securing information for so many things that they were taking four, five, or six books from the school library, plus those from the public library. The reading program never ended at any one time period. Instead, it acted as a springboard for daily, weekly. and yearly class activities in all subject areas. (p. 5)

Deborah Weiner (1985) used the model with in-service teachers as a laboratory requirement. They analyzed their lesson plans and the results according to Bloom's (1956) taxonomy and found that more of the higher levels of thinking resulted than when the taxonomy itself was used to plan the lessons.

CONCLUSION

The development of the ten rational processes proposed by the Educational Policies Commission as the central purpose of American education is a worthwhile goal. However, in the light of present-day information and the requirements of the future information society, the ten rational processes are not enough. The ten rational processes must be complemented by processes that go beyond the rational processes and result in creative thinking and the solution of problems that cannot be solved by traditional logical thinking. Since the proposal of the Educational Policies Commission in 1961, there have been many important developments in this area and these should be considered in today's education. We have proposed a three-stage model of instruction that may be used as a guide in planning courses, planning lessons, developing instructional materials, and in making instruction more effective. The results have been excellent and we believe it will be effective in teaching gifted and talented children in the regular classroom.

10

Creative Reading

ALTHOUGH the information given in the preceding chapter on the Incubation Model of Teaching can be applied to reading, creative reading is so important in teaching gifted and talented children in the regular classroom, that additional suggestions and procedures will be described in this chapter.

Even creatively gifted children need help in becoming creative readers. Children not creatively gifted but gifted in other ways may need a great deal of help in becoming creative readers. Children who have been overtrained in becoming critical readers or in reading to absorb and remember all of the facts also may have difficulty in becoming creative readers. It takes effort and practice to shift from critical or retention reading to creative reading. Then after a child begins reading creatively, there are a number of skills that need further development. In this chapter, some of these skills will be identified and ways for developing them will be outlined. The kind of reading involved here may include not only basic readers, literature books, and outside readings but also readings in history, geography, science, mathematics, and other subjects. All fields can provide experiences in creative thinking.

WHY READING CREATIVELY IS IMPORTANT

Even in giving children a realistic view of the world through their reading, it is necessary that they read creatively. Only in this way can they grasp the sights, sounds, smells, and tactile sensations of the world. Only by using their imagination can the movements and actions of the world become real. Only if they are read creatively can books become a source of thinking materials in solving problems and coping with life's stresses. Only the creative reader is able to ferret out the truth from what is reads. It takes a creative reader to remember in a meaningful way what is read.

Almost all courses in memory improvement make a special point of calling imagination into play.

Besides its use in acquiring a realistic view of the world, reading should be a source of materials for use in solving problems. Our ability to think is limited primarily by our personal experiences and the uses we make of them in problem solving, in abstracting and generalizing, in judging, and in making decisions. Creative readers increase their store of personal experiences through reading because they use the ideas gained as they would firsthand experiences. In solving problems and reaching decisions they are as likely to see the relevance of story situations or biographical accounts as they are the relevance of firsthand experiences. What they read becomes real to them and they can use it.

Ferreting out the truth from what one reads requires that one be both a critical and creative reader. Being a critical reader only makes a child aware of the biases and deficiencies in the accounts of writers. It takes a creative reader to understand the reasons behind discrepant accounts and to reach sound conclusions about what is true.

It is apparently not the amount of information one possesses that enables one to think creatively, solve problems, and reach sound decisions, but rather the way the information is stored and our attitude toward it.

WHAT IT MEANS TO READ CREATIVELY

In a number of experiments the first author has tried to describe some of the essentials of reading creatively. For example, the following instructions were given in an experiment involving the use of different reading sets in mastering textbook assignments (Torrance & Harmon, 1961):

When you read, it is important that you think about the many possible uses of the information which you are reading. It is especially important that you think of the various ways in which the information could be used in your personal and professional life. In reading, do not just ask, "What is the author saying?" Also ask, "How can I use what the author is saying?" Do not stop with just one use. Think of as many uses as you can of the important ideas presented. Jot down some of their uses for future reference or action. It may take some practice before you are really successful in assuming this set or attitude towards your reading, but do not be discouraged. By the third day, you should find it easy to assume this set.

The results of this study indicated rather clearly that the way in which information is stored makes a great deal of difference in how it will be used. You might want to practice this set, or attitude, in reading the remainder of this chapter or some other reading assignment.

In the experiment involving the critical and creative reading of research reports, those reading the reports with a critical set were required to describe the defects in the statement of the problem and its importance, the underlying assumptions and hypotheses studied, procedures for collecting and analyzing data, the conclusions and interpretations of the findings, and a critical appraisal of the worth of the research. The creative readers were asked to think of new possibilities suggested by the statement of the problem, other possible hypotheses related to the problem and its solution, improvements which could have been made in collecting and analyzing the data, other possible conclusions and interpretations of the findings, and an appraisal of the possibilities stemming from the findings. In projects given after this experience, students who had read the research reports creatively produced new ideas of their own which were judged to be more creative than were those of their peers who read critically.

There are a number of ways to describe what happens when students read creatively. One way is through the use of the definition the first author has proposed for creativity: When students read creatively, they are sensitive to problems and possibilities in whatever they read. They make themselves aware of the gaps in knowledge, the unsolved problems, the missing elements, things that are incomplete or out of focus. To resolve this tension, so important in the creative thinking process, creative readers see new relationships, create new combinations, synthesize relatively unrelated elements into a coherent whole, redefine or transform certain pieces of information to discover new uses, and build onto what is known. In this search for solutions, they produce a large number of possibilities, use a great variety of strategies or approaches, look at the available information in a variety of ways, break away from commonplace solutions into bold new ways, and develop ideas by filling in the details and making the idea attractive and exciting to others

In order for these things to happen in the process of reading, readers must be open to their experiences and reflect upon what they read, discovering relationships among the ideas presented, evaluating them in the light of their experiences. They must be able to play with the possibility that the new idea might be useful and try to envision what its consequences might be. Thus, the new idea becomes a center of vivid, concrete images and feeling reactions. They must have an inquiring attitude about what they read. Frequently, they try to identify with the author so that they can grasp what the author had in mind, so that they can predict what the author is going to say next.

HOW CREATIVE READERS DEVELOP

Teachers can help children become creative readers in two major ways. First they can do things to help heighten the child's expectations and anticipation as a reading task is approached. Second they can permit or encourage children to do something with what is read, either at the time it is being read or afterwards.

HEIGHTENING EXPECTATION
AND ANTICIPATION

The creative process itself embodies the tension of anticipation or expectation, and individuals who distinguish themselves in artistic, scientific, and entrepreneurial creation exemplify this tension quite vividly. It has variously been described as the warming up process, the ability to rise to the occasion, or attraction to the unknown, the strange, and the puzzling.

Teachers of gifted and talented children will be able to think of materials and methods for heightening the tension of expectation from kindergarten through graduate school. A few examples of such materials and methods will be offered.

One of the first author's favorite sets of material at the preschool and primary levels is a series of books by Bruno Munari, an Italian artist and storyteller; they include *Who's There? Open the Door* (1957), *The Elephant's Wish* (1959a), and *The Birthday Present* (1959b). *The Elephant's Wish* is especially useful in developing imaginatively the concept and skills of empathy. The story begins: "The elephant is bored with being a big heavy animal. He wishes he could be something else. What do you think he would like to be?" This starts the empathic guessing game. The child is asked to look into the mind of the elephant, imaginatively to put himself in the place of the elephant, and think what he/she would do if he/she were tired of being an elephant. Then the child is given a look into the elephant's mind by the artist-author through the clever device of a flap on the elephant's head, which can be pulled back. "He wishes he could be a little bird who flies and sings." The bird, however, has his problems. "The little bird is bored with flying and singing. He is wishing too. What does he wish?" After some guessing on his part, the child can be given a look into the bird's mind. The story continues with the fish, a lizard, and a fat, lazy ox. The ox wants to be an elephant, illustrating the need for reacting to limitations creatively rather than cynically and using whatever abilities and resources we have.

Somewhat the same effect can be obtained when reading new material in the primary and intermediate grades by asking, before you turn the page in the middle of a story, "What do you think will happen now?" Later you can encourage children to ask questions that will lead them to find relationships among certain facts and thus come to a logical conclusions. This same technique can be given enough facts to enable them to make predictions and then asked to make guesses about the consequences. Later the students can check their guesses against documentary sources or established facts and try to determine wherein their theorizing went wrong.

The first author has used this technique in some of the experimental materials created and tested in the fourth grade. In these materials the atmosphere of expectation is created through brief dramas of great moments of scientific and geographical discovery and historical achievement, as well as fantasies. An example from the fantasy series is our use of the famous Italian story *Giovanni and the Giant* (Cunnington & Torrance, 1965). In the dramatization the tape recorder is stopped each time Giovanni gets himself into a predicament. The students are asked to think of as many solutions as possible for extricating Giovanni. By the time the tape is completed, each student has enough material for another version of the story. After this kind of experience pupils may be invited to expand the story or put it into a here-and-now setting. Or they may be invited to write newspaper articles dealing with selected parts of the story from an "I-was-there" viewpoint. This, in turn, can lead to reading creatively more material about twelfth-century Italy, the Crusades, city-states, and the like.

In the intermediate grades and in the high-school years something of the same effect can be achieved by giving the title of a book and asking students to guess what the book is about. Josephine Shotka (1961) has suggested a list of questions which can be used to stimulate creative reading. They are designed for stories but can be adapted to biographies, history, and other kinds of reading materials. Here are some of the questions she suggests for use before the story is read:

- From the name of the story, what do you think it will be like?
- What experiences do you think the characters will have?
- Do you think this will be a funny story, a sad story, a make-believe story, or an exciting story? Why?
- What do you think the characters will be like?

The following is a sample of the questions she suggests for use during the reading of the story:

- Why did you like or dislike the story?
- What would you have done if you were in the same position as the character or characters of the story?
- How do you think the character or characters felt? Have you ever felt like this?

The use of such questions emphasizes the fact that reading creatively involves reactions to the reading material before, during, and after the actual reading. Then there is still the matter of doing something further with what has been read. One of the major problems in arousing anticipation and expectation is to lead the reader to see the fundamental relationships among the facts, ideas, and events that constitute the reading material and between them and the experiences and problems of the reader.

DOING SOMETHING WITH WHAT IS READ

The first author was amazed when he began giving examinations that require that students do something with the theories and research findings they had studied. One device used was to give important research findings and ask students to list all of the educational uses they could think of for these findings. Student after student would come to him and say, "What do you mean by 'uses'? The only thing that I can think of is to tell it to somebody." This experience helped the first author begin understanding why courses in education, psychology, and the other behavioral sciences have so little impact on what happens in classrooms. Students were struggling with courses and learning facts that they did not intend ever to use. Indeed it had not occurred to them that such information could be useful in any very concrete or real sense! Some ways by which creative readers can be developed by "doing something with what is read" will be outlined now.

1. ***Reproducing What Is Read with Imagination.*** Even if one's goal is only to "tell it to someone," as in the case of the first author's Educational Psychology students, it can be done with imagination. If you have difficulty in getting pupils to read orally with imagination, John Ciardi (1962) might help you in this task. The first author has been fascinated by Ciardi's recording *I Met a Man* by Pathways of Sound, Inc. This recording grew out of Ciardi's attempt to teach his own daughter how to read with meaning and imagination when she was in the first grade. His aim in the recording is to encourage children to put meaning into their reading instead of mouthing the words, whether the mouthing be slow or rapid. He encourages the young reader to make poems "sound like the thing happening."

2. ***Elaborating What Is Read.*** Next to reproducing what is read comes elaborating what is read. There are many ways of elaborating upon what one reads and thus developing creative readers. Durrell and Chambers (1958) predicted that "it will probably be found that well-designed exercises in elaborative thinking in reading will produce higher permanent retention and greater availability of knowledge to new situations." One of the most common means of doing this is to have children illustrate what they read. Other media such as music, songs, rhythmic movement, and dramatics can also be used in elaborating what has been read. Also valuable are modifications of what is read: writing a different ending, changing a character in some specific way and seeing what else this would change, expanding upon a certain episode in a story.

   Some children who are having difficulty in learning to read will probably learn to do so, if given experiences in elaborating what is read. An illustrative case is one reported by Joy Alice Holm (Torrance, 1962a pp. 176-7). Bob was a miserable and withdrawn junior-high-school student. As a high-school student he was considered a hopeless case because he could not read. Throughout elementary school, Bob's teachers had called him "sweet but dumb." Now he was too miserable to be "sweet." Bob was in Holm's English class and also in her art class. She worked with him on his reading after school, and he illustrated the stories the class read. Holm writes that Bob's illustrations showed that he understood the thoughts and he transformed them into vivid pictures. Since he could neither write about the meaning and details of a poem or story nor talk about them, Holm permitted him to take his tests by illustrating the stories the class had read. Other students were amazed at the depth of meaning that he showed them through his illustrations. Finally, after almost a year of illustrating his way through English class and drawing and painting away many of his conflicts, he increased his reading skill and participated again in sports.

There are a number of remarkable facets of Holm's encounter with Bob. She was willing to embark with him on an untrodden path. What teacher would have thought of letting Bob take his English examinations using figural or visual rather than verbal symbols? Most teachers would be afraid that they could not "grade" or "correct" such an examination paper. By "going along" in this unorthodox fashion, a "hopeless case" learned to read and perhaps escape a life of pathological withdrawal.

This example is offered for two reasons. The technique of elaborating what is read through means other than words may be useful in reaching some slow gifted students and enabling them to achieve some of their potentialities. It is also offered because many parents and teachers believe that a child must first be a *good reader* before he/she can be a creative reader. The authors would maintain, however, that a child is not a good reader unless he/she is also a creative reader.

For the gifted child, however, work in elaborating what is read will have its greatest usefulness in developing the ability to relate the content of reading to previous knowledge, produce illustrations and applications, practice using what has been read, relate what has been read to other fields, and make associations that integrate reading into action. Durrell and Chambers (1958) suggest that elaborative thinking in connection with reading may be better done in groups of various sizes than in either individual or whole-class activities. They also suggest that specific planning or applications are better than remote or academic tasks and that intensive sequential instruction is more effective than occasional or incidental instruction. This is very similar to our suggestion for procedures that permit one activity to lead to another, making use of the power of the "warm-up" process in producing readiness for kinds of learning that would otherwise be unlikely.

3. *Transforming and Rearranging What Is Read.* Third in the first author's scale of doing something with what is read is the transformation or rearrangement of what is read. Shakespeare's creativity was of this type. It probably never occurred to Shakespeare that a playwright should invent a plot and characters. With all of the great stories in history, science, geography, and government — with all of the myths and fables available, with all of the great biographies — there are plenty of plots and characters waiting to be brought to life in dramas, songs, paintings, murals, and other forms by creative readers. Of course, in bringing these plots and characters to life in such a way, students will need to read creatively from a number of sources. What results will be a creative recombination and transformation of what has been read.

The book report assignment or report on other outside reading can also be made a transformation of what has been read. Mauree Applegate (1962) and others have given an exciting variety of suggestions for such assignments. The following are some of Applegate's suggestions:

1. What was your favorite character like? Make a drawing and point out passages in the story which make you think this is the way your character looks.

2. Before you read the book, write the story the title makes you think of; then when you read the book, write the report of the real story and chuckle at the difference. (You may feel that you have a better story.)

3. Write an interview between a character in the book and the author, between you and the author, between two characters in the book, between you and a character in the book, or between you and a friend about the book.

4. Write your book report in reverse.

5. You have just finished reading a biography. Pretend you visited the person when he/she was your age. Tell about the fun you had.

6. Choose a lively scene from a book you and your friends have read and either dramatize it or make a puppet play of it.

7. Have a friend interview you about a book of which you pretend to be the author.

8. Make a hand-rolled movie of a book you have read.

9. Make a radio or television play of your favorite book.

Teachers of gifted and talented children will be able to think of many others that are even more exciting than the ones Applegate suggests. With little prodding, gifted and talented children themselves will invent an astounding array of ideas.

4. *Going Beyond What Is Read.* In the creative process, one thing must be permitted to lead to another. Creativity begets creativity. A good story is likely to evoke many ideas and questions which will send the reader beyond the story. Going beyond a basic reader story or great literary work is a natural and integral part of all group-directed reading.

The idea of permitting one thing to lead to another is the very essence of the experimental materials the first author has produced. Basic to this strategy is generating enthusiasm, interest, and curiosity through the tape-recorded drama and then using this warm-up to get pupils to produce something. They are then encouraged to produce something on the basis of what they have already produced. Additional reading may come in at any one of several stages in the process, and we believe that such reading is almost certain to be creative reading. Let us examine an example from one of the lessons based on *Eyes at Their Fingertips*, the story of Louis Braille (Cunnington, Myers, Buckland, and Peterson, 1962). The instructions for the first step go something like the following:

One of the big reasons Louis Braille thought of and worked out a way for blind people to read and write better was that the old way really bothered him. It really got under his skin that little blind children had to read out of books that were so big that they couldn't carry them around. And besides, reading raised or embossed writing wasn't very accurate. Try to think of as many things as you can that really bother you and get on your nerves — things that bother you so much that you would like to change them or invent something new to make them less annoying. List as many of them as you can.

Immediately after this list has been produced, we go ahead to the second stage with the following instructions:

Of all the things you listed, what bothers you most? What really gets you down? Is there any one of the things you listed on the first page that towers over all of the others and makes them seem small? Pick out one of the things you have just listed and write it down.

Then follows:

Now think of all of the things that you can about this annoyance, or "thorn in your flesh," that make it annoying and list them below. What is there about it that bothers you?

After this pupils are told:

Now list as many things as you can think of that would make it less annoying or remove the annoyance from your life. It doesn't have to be something that is now possible. Play being a magician and list all of the things that would make it ideal.

After thinking this through, they are then asked to continue with the following instructions:

Now think of something that you could invent or some plan that would remove some of the things that bother you about this annoyance and would have as many as possible of the characteristics that you just listed.

After this we definitely have a phase that calls for creative reading. The orientation for this is as follows:

Louis Braille was helped in developing his kind of writing because he was familiar with sonography which had proven unsuccessful. Do you know of any unsuccessful attempts to solve the problem you selected? If you do, write them below. If you don't know of any, how could you find out if there have been any?

The next phase is introduced as follows:

If you thought of some unsuccessful attempt to solve your problem, what would have to be changed about it to make it successful?

Following this step pupils are encouraged to draw a picture or diagram of the invention, plan, or procedure that they have in mind or to describe it as fully as possible. As a final step they are asked to think of the possible consequences of their invention or plan. This activity is introduced in the following words:

If you were to succeed with your invention or plan, it would change many things. Think of as many things as you can that would probably be changed, if your invention or plan becomes successful.

It will be noted that an effort has been made to reproduce essentially the same thinking process Louis Braille pursued in working out a system of writing and reading for the blind. In each of the great moments of discovery, an effort is made to distill in the drama as much as possible the essence of the thinking of the scientist or inventor. Benjamin Franklin's thinking processes were motivated in quite a different way from Braille's. He was sensitive to the needs of other people and he kept inventing and suggesting things that would solve problems for other people — for example, bifocals, lightning rods, coal stoves, mail-delivery service, police and fire departments, political cartoons, Poor Richard sayings, street lights, and the like. Thus, instead of starting with personal concerns with the Benjamin Framklin story, we start children by having them observe what things bother other people. In this way children are brought back again and again to read creatively.

CONCLUSION

Since most gifted and talented children are avid readers, guidance that will improve their skills as creative readers is especially promising and might influence performance in all areas of the curriculum. The Incubation Model was initially devised for use in teaching all children to read creatively. However, since creative reading is so important in teaching gifted and talented children in the regular classroom, additional suggestions and procedures have been described. There are skills that need to be further developed. Some of these skills are identified and ways of developing them have been outlined and what it means to read creatively was explained. The importance of encouraging children to do something with what is read was emphasized.

11

Developing Research Concepts And Skills

T HE AUTHORS have long been advocates of teaching children research concepts and skills as early as possible. We believe that it is important for children to know how to find out. Again, this is an excellent vehicle for teaching gifted and talented children in the regular classroom.

When the first author began talking about his experience in teaching gifted sixth-grade pupils concepts and skills in doing research, most of his colleagues regarded his accounts as fantasy. Even after he and Myers produced a monograph and an article about the 1961 experiences in *Gifted Child Quarterly* (Torrance and Myers, 1962ab), few people took these accounts seriously. As time has passed, he has been reassured by many teachers that his experiences in teaching research concepts and skills to elementary pupils can be replicated by intelligent and imaginative teachers. Other colleagues found the materials contained in the monograph useful in teaching high-school and college undergraduates research concepts and skills. Whenever the first author has met the parents of the students who had been in these early classes several years afterwards, they almost always report spontaneously that their children were still using the research concepts and skills learned in the sixth grade in school and out-of-school activities. Thus, research concepts learned in the sixth grade had become tools in future learning and thinking.

Since research has become increasingly complex, it is not strange that people would believe that teaching gifted elementary-school children concepts and skills of doing research is fantasy. The teaching of research concepts and skills has almost always been reserved for the graduate-school period, especially in education. Furthermore, there has been a tendency in some graduate schools to eliminate the teaching of research concepts and skills from the first year of graduate work. Discussions on teaching elementary students how to do research are usually limited to procedures for "looking something up in the library" and rarely touch upon the methods and concepts of creative scientific research.

PROMISING DEVELOPMENTS

Already there are a number of experiences that indicate that elementary and high-school students have a great readiness for research and can achieve very worthwhile results, when given a chance. Quite exciting has been Jablonski's work at the University of Pittsburgh (Guilford, 1962a; Taylor, 1964c). Jablonski discovered the potential of gifted high-school students participating in National Science Foundation Summer Science Programs. He encouraged his summer proteges to continue their research work the year round and solicited the help of personnel in the Pittsburgh schools. Some of the student experiments have been published in regular professional journals against the competition of mature and experienced scientists. Jablonski estimates that 25 per cent of his high-school researchers have produced publishable material.

Jablonski wanted next to begin working with younger students. His colleagues told him that this was really getting ridiculous, but nevertheless he went ahead with projects with fourth-, fifth-, and sixth grade students. Jablonski admits that he had grossly underestimated the readiness of these children to do research. Groups of them joined him in cancer research. They asked the meaning of words and soon mastered the technical language just as if they were learning English. As a result, these youngsters produced useful research ideas and discoveries.

Over the years since Jablonski's work, there have continued to be accounts of achievements similar to those of Jabolonski's proteges. An individual success story is that of Bracie Watson, a gifted black boy in Alabama (1968 International Fair) who won top place in the 1968 International Science Fair. When Bracie was a high school junior, his teacher arranged a mentorship for him with one of the scientists at the University of Alabama Medical Center. He won the state science fair championship. In his senior year, he continued working at the Alabama Medical Center on his senior year science fair project. He proved that baby mice could be kept alive in an artificial womb.

A highly successful group experience in the medical science area has been described by Shepherd (1972). This experiment has been known as the High School Education Program at the University of Pennsylvania, shortened to HEP-UP. The initial program involved thirty students, ten each from three large high schools near the university. These students were selected on the basis of high motivation, but not necessarily high achievement. The project directors, however, were looking for youngsters who might have good science grades or might be "turned on" to science. Many surprising successes followed, although some of those selected were "too filled with tension and hatred to work in the situation." In an evaluation of the project, the evidence described by Shepherd indicates that black economically disadvantaged youngsters can be competitive with the more affluent students in medical schools and graduate schools.

For some time we have believed that most research concepts and many research skills can be taught to elementary students, especially gifted ones. We have been convinced too that if gifted students can be taught these concepts and skills at an early age, they will have available some very powerful tools to aid them in their learning and thinking from that time onward. This makes learning more exciting and the search for "truth" more rewarding.

In 1959-60, the first author tested this idea in part through a five-day course taught to the High Achievers Class, a class of carefully selected gifted sixth-graders, in Bloomington, Minnesota. For several years the course was repeated and varied. The course as described herein may suggest quite different ideas to different teachers. Some may want to expand the program and others may wish to select individual concepts from it. The examples of problems and projects should be regarded only as illustrations.

NEW DEVELOPMENTS IN TEACHING STATISTICS AND RESEARCH CONCEPTS

There have been recent developments in teaching statistics, research concepts, and procedures to elementary school children. Textbooks and instructional materials have been created by Technical Education Research Centers and Lesley College (Corwin & Friel, 1990; Friel, Mokros, & Russell, 1992; Russell & Corwin, 1989). Russell and Corwin's book is for teaching children in grades 4-6 how to collect real data in the classroom and to compute and interpret statistics to test hypotheses. Corwin and Friel's book is designed to teach children in grades 5-6 the concepts and skills of prediction and sampling. Friel, Mokros, and Russell's book is designed for teaching measures of central tendency and variability also to children in grades 5-6.

These authors argue in the preface of each of these books that in "an information-rich society such as ours, statistics are an increasingly important aspect of daily life." Japan has long recognized this and has made statistics an integral part of the elementary school curriculum. The first author observed a group of 3-5 grade children working on a problem in which they had generated data about the health practices of habits of the children in the school. They had already collected the data and were engaged in processing these data and computing the statistics. The plan was for this group of fifteen children to interpret the results and prepare a report to all of the children in the school, their teachers and parents. It would then be discussed in the school and home.

Sisk noted that her sixth grade gifted students in California were highly curious about her involvement and enthusiasm in her noon time studies of statistics for a graduate educational psychology course. The students were not only curious, but they were eager to learn about these research methods. Sisk mentioned the students' interest to her professor and he grinned, and tongue in cheek suggested that the students be introduced to the terminology and material. The gifted students approached the noon time study excitedly. Later in the semester at the professor's request, ten of the students attended the evening class. They confidently approached the chalkboard, computed means, modes and medians to the classroom teachers amazement. They fielded questions on establishing control groups and the importance of tests of significance.

The final exam in the graduate course consisted of one comprehensive problem in which the student either passed or failed in computing the standard deviation. The professor agreed that the elementary students could take the exam. All ten of the gifted students passed the exam, whereas only 22 of the 25 teachers passed the exam. As a result of the gifted students' eagerness and success with research and statistics, this component was added to the curriculum for sixth grade gifted students in Garden Grove, California.

Corwin, Friel, Mokros, and Russell report that the Curriculum and Evaluation Standards for School Mathematics is now stressing the importance of incorporating data analysis into the elementary mathematics curriculum to prepare children for living and working in a world filled with information based on data. They argue that children of all ages are interested in real data regarding themselves and the world around them.

These authors also point out in their prefaces (Russell & Corwin, 1989, p. 1) that "As students engage in the study of statistics, they, like scientists and statisticians, participate in:
- cooperative learning
- theory building
- discussing and defining terms and procedures
- dealing with uncertainty.

"We want elementary school students to have an opportunity to engage in such real mathematical behavior, discussing, describing, challenging each other, and building theories about real-world phenomena based on their work."

AN ILLUSTRATIVE EXPERIENCE: THE COURSE FOR GIFTED SIXTH-GRADERS

The class with which the course was developed (Torrance & Myers, 1962) consisted of 46 pupils selected on the basis of achievement and intelligence (minimum Stanford-Binet IQ, 135). Each morning students functioned as two separate classes under different teachers. During this period they followed essentially the same curriculum as other sixth-grade classes, except that they had lessons in French. This left the afternoons free for other ventures. On alternate weeks they worked on their "strengths and weaknesses" under the direction of their teachers. During the other weeks both groups studied for a week with "alter teachers" — experts in some special field such as medicine, journalism, art music, psychology, architecture, politics. The course on "how to do research" was offered as a part of the alter-teacher program.

MAJOR OBJECTIVES OF THE COURSE

The course was presented to the High Achievers Class as one in educational research. Its major objectives were:

1. To familiarize gifted elementary students with some of the more powerful concepts of research in the behavioral sciences, in order that these concepts might become tools in their learning early in their educational careers,

2. To communicate to gifted students the excitement of doing original research, exploring the unknown and pushing forward knowledge,

3. To provide experiences in participating in educational research and in conducting and reporting experiments with real consequences,

4. To develop in gifted elementary students some skills in formulating hypotheses, testing them, and in reporting the results,

5. To aid gifted elementary students in the further development of their self-concepts by making them aware of some of their own creative thinking processes and abilities.

LESSON ONE: What Is Research?

The first session began with an exploration of the concept of "research." Some students defined it as a "way of digging into things." Others associated "research" with "experimenting" and others with "looking things up in books." Some defined it as a way of "finding out the truth about things that you don't know or nobody knows." Using the materials that were offered, it was concluded that there are many things we do not know — that no one knows — and that we can find out many of the things we do not know by a more or less formal, systematic, intensive process of carrying on the scientific method.

What's in the Box?

Following this preliminary exploration of the general nature of research, the "What's-in-the-Box" game was used to give the High Achievers an opportunity to develop a concept of the research process through a personal experience. The pupils were shown two boxes. They all agreed that none of them really knew what was in either of the boxes. The two classes were then invited to enter into a contest to see which could find out what was in one of the boxes. Classes returned to their rooms which were just across the hall from one another, one working with the first author and the other with R. E. Myers.

In both groups, the students were told that the object in the box was round. They were then invited to make several wild guesses of round things which might be in the box. They agreed, however, that at this point no one really knew which of the guesses was correct or whether any of them were correct. When asked to find out what was in the box without opening it, they immediately wanted to experiment — to lift the box, shake it, smell it, and otherwise examine it. One group found that the object inside the box made no sound and was quite light. They immediately eliminated all objects that would make a sound or would be heavy. Some said that there was an odor; others could detect no odor. No one could specifically identify the odor.

The other group found that the object in its box made a sound, was light, and was apparently quite small as it rattled around very easily. No one could detect any odor. This group then eliminated soft objects, heavy objects, large objects, and objects having strong odors. Thus, they eliminated the kinds of objects the first group had retained and kept the kinds of objects it had eliminated.

After eliminating obviously incorrect hypotheses, each group made new hypotheses, or guesses, and started asking questions which could be answered by "yes" or "no." They eliminated the guesses one by one and finally hit upon the correct identity — in one case, a powder puff, in the other, a Sucret (cough drop). This was then verified by opening the boxes and examining the objects.

The persons who identified the objects correctly then described the process of *synthesis* by which they arrived at the correct answer. Others described the process by which they had arrived at incorrect guesses near the end of the process and tried to identify what they thought had "thrown them off."

In summarizing the experience, the class identified the following steps in the process:

1. Recognizing that you don't know something.

2. Making wild guesses (multiple hypotheses) on the basis of available information (general appearance).

3. Closer examination and observation, experimenting, testing.
4. Eliminating obviously incorrect guesses on basis of additional information.
5. Making "better" guesses in the light of new information.
6. Asking questions to test guesses (hypotheses).
7. Eliminating incorrect guesses on basis of additional information.
8. Making "closer" guesses, sythesizing accumulated information.
9. Verifying final answer.

At each step, an effort was made to relate the experiences of group members to research concepts.

Three Kinds of Research

After drawing conclusions concerning the steps in the process of research, they were told that these steps might be carried out in any one of three kinds of research: historical, descriptive, and experimental. Each type was discussed briefly.

LESSON TWO: An Experience in Historiography

A Personal Problem in Historical Research

An attempt was made to establish a beginning for the development of the concepts of historical research through the use of a personal problem. Near the end of the first session the High Achievers were given the first of the "How-Did-You-Grow?" exercises. They were asked to make guesses, or estimates, concerning the trends in their development from first through sixth grade in the following eight characteristics, in the form of developmental curves:

- shoe size;
- height;
- curiosity;
- reading speed;
- imagination;
- spelling;
- independence in thinking;
- arithmetic computation.

Each student was given a set of the same charts they had just filled out and told to collect all of the data they could to test the trends they had already hypothesized. Before trying to recall specific information or to collect any information, they were asked to list on the booklet all of the ways they could think of to check their guesses. Some of these were discussed briefly. They were also asked to record what information they could recall or collect relevant to each of the eight aspects of development.

The Experience in Historical Research

The next day, the High Achievers reported a great variety of sources of information used in trying to establish their developmental curves more accurately. They discovered that these sources could be classified either as "records" or as "witnesses."

The experiences were related to the concepts of historical research. One of the first problems introduced by them was that of "bias." They asked, "What do you do when witnesses tell you just the opposite?" This was identified as the problem of "bias." Several indicated that their mothers had said that they were very curious when they were young, but that they had become less curious as they grew older. Their fathers, however, said that they had shown little evidence of curiosity until the past two or three years. They were then asked to think of the kinds of observations their mothers might have made and of the kinds of observations their fathers might have made. From this they were able to formulate several hypotheses concerning the reasons for the discrepancies in the conclusions of their mothers and fathers. Apparently mothers have more contacts with their children during their early years than do fathers and are naturally more aware of their curiosity tendencies. As mothers gradually discourage their question asking, become unable or refuse to answer their questions, children turn increasingly to their fathers.

The "frame of reference" was also a frequent problem. In a number of instances many made their estimates in quantitative terms such as shoe size, feet and inches, words per minute, spelling words added, and the like. Some established their frame of reference in terms of their peers; others did year-by-year comparisons with themselves.

LESSON THREE:
An Experience in Descriptive Research

To generate a set of data for use in a descriptive study, the High Achievers were administered the Ask-and-Guess Test. A Mother Goose print of Mother Hubbard was used as the stimulus material. The print shows Mother Hubbard opening the cupboard which is completely bare and the dog looking at the empty cupboard. The following general orientation was given for the task:

One good way of finding out things that we don't know is to ask questions. To get the information we want, we have to ask the right questions. Sometimes we can't find out by asking questions, so we have to make the best guesses we can. Then, whenever we can, we try to find out if our guesses are correct. The three tasks which we shall do now will give you a chance to show how good you are at asking questions and making guesses to find out things.

They were first instructed to produce as many questions as they could think of concerning the events depicted. Next they were asked to formulate hypotheses about the possible causes of the events and finally they were asked to formulate hypotheses about possible consequences.

Upon completion of the Ask-and-Guess Test (Torrance, 1962a), the High Achievers were confronted with the problem of devising ways of quantifying and describing their performance on the three tasks that they had just completed. They decided that one way to describe their performance would be to count the number of questions, causes, and consequences produced. They were asked then to do this. In counting the number of questions asked, they were cautioned not to count any questions that could have been answered by looking at the picture. In the case of "causes" they were asked to check to see if each response made some hypothesis about causation and to eliminate responses that were merely sequences of events that might have occurred before the action. In the case of "consequences" the same type of check was suggested.

They decided that one way to describe the group would be to add the number of responses to each of the parts for all of the class and divide it by the number who took the test. They were told that this was known in statistics as the "mean" and was a "measure of central tendency." They were asked how else we might describe some central tendency of the group. Someone suggested that the score of the middle ranked person might be used. The instructor identified this as the "median." They were also told that another useful way of describing a group is to determine the typical or "modal," performance, the score made by the largest number of people. They were then asked to determine the mean, median, and mode of their own scores which had been placed on the blackboard.

Someone suggested that the highest and lowest scores would also help in describing their performance and noted that scores on the "Ask" part ran from 5 to 19, "Causes" from 0 to 17, "Consequences" from 5 to 22, and total scores from 14 to 51. This was identified as the "range," a measure of the way in which they vary. (Since the data as arranged did not suggest a clear illustration of other measures of variability, no effort was made at this point to develop further the concepts of variance, standard deviation, and the like.)

It was then suggested that they might describe their performance more completely and meaningfully by comparisons within their own group and between their group and some other groups. They then obtained the means and medians for boys and girls separately. It was noted that both the means and medians for the girls were higher than those of the boys on all three scores and the total. They were then confronted with the problem of whether the differences are great enough to be accepted with confidence or if they might have occurred by chance. Some did not believe that the differences were large enough to amount to anything and that boys might do as well or better than girls, if given the same or a similar task. They were then introduced to the concept of levels of confidence and the use of the *t* test to determine the level of confidence of differences in means.

Tests of significance were made by the author and reported to the class the next day, all three being significant at better than the 5 per cent level.

It was pointed out that comparing a group with some other groups is an aid in describing performance. As a matter of interest, the following comparative data were compiled from other studies:

Comparison Group	Questions	Causes	Conseq.	Means Totals
High Achievers	10.86	8.45	12.52	31.84
Regular sixth grade in suburban school	7.59	4.70	5.30	17.59
Twelfth grade at University High School	10.86	7.24	10.34	27.96
Graduate students in Educational Psychology 159	13.35	8.71	11.40	33.46
Nursing students, Seniors	10.80	8.07	9.60	28.47

It was apparent from these data that the High Achievers performed considerably better than a regular sixth grade class in the area, as well or better than twelfth-grade students at University High School and nursing students at a local diploma school, and almost as well as graduate students in the author's class in Educational Psychology. It was cautioned that we would have to compute tests of significance before we could determine the confidence to be placed in the observed differences.

Time did not permit the development of the concept of variability as thoroughly in the present course as in the earlier ones. In earlier courses, scores on the *Things Done Check List*, a list of 243 science activities, were used as the basis for developing concepts of descriptive statistics. With these data the concept of variance is more obvious and is usually grasped spontaneously. Someone noted, "Boys are more variable in the number of activities they checked. See, some of the boys are higher than any of the girls and some of them are lower than any of the girls. The girls are in a kind of narrow band."

A longer allotment of time would have been helpful. With a little instruction, however, there is no reason why pupils cannot compute means, tests of significance, and standard deviations. We believe, however, that the important thing is that gifted students grasp the concepts, and they do this readily.

LESSON FOUR: An Experience in Quantification

The dependence of research upon quantification, or measurement, was discussed briefly. It was pointed out that scientific advances in some areas are blocked until problems of measurement can be solved. When measurement problems are solved, there is frequently of flood of research, and rapid progress in the field follows. Examples of quantification were pointed out in the historical and descriptive studies already conducted.

Since the High Achievers had been assigned to write an imaginative story for their homework, the problem of quantifying their stories was considered. The stories assigned for this purpose concerned animals and persons with divergent characteristics, such as *The Lion That Would Not Roar, The Flying Monkey, The Man Who Cries,* and the like.

Quantification of Stories

It was pointed out that some of the characteristics of their stories were easy to quantify objectively, but that others would require more thinking. They readily listed those that could be quantified objectively. These included:

- number of words;
- number of sentences;
- number of paragraphs;
- number writing on each topic;
- number who made up their own topics;
- amount of time required to write the stories;
- number of words misspelled and percentage of words misspelled;
- number of errors in punctuation;
- number of errors in capitalization;
- number of action words;
- number having happy endings.

It was agreed that once numbers had been assigned to these characteristics, we could then apply concepts such as mean, median, mode, range, and the like.

The class was then asked to identify other qualities of stories that might be useful in describing their stories or testing hypotheses about them.

They then concluded that it would be valuable if we could quantify the "interest" the stories generated in the reader, their originality, and their content.

Concerning the quantification of "interest," the class suggested that consideration be given to such things as the use of surprise, humor, the personal element, and the like. Similarly they discussed signs that might be used in quantifying "originality." They suggested such things as unusual solution or ending, surprise, unusual setting or plot, invented words or names, picturesque or colorful words or expressions, and the like. It was suggested that a story could be checked for the absence or presence of these qualities and a rough measure or estimate could be determined thereby.

Attention was then turned to the analysis of content. Since all of the stories involved some divergent characteristic of an animal or person, it was then suggested that we might center our analysis on the handling of the divergent characteristic (what made them different). Since the first author had developed such a system, categories already developed were used so that the High Achievers could compare their stories with those written by children in other countries. They were shown stories written on the same topics by children in India, Turkey, Greece, France, and Germany. They were then shown how they could compare the characteristics of their stories with those of children in the other countries. Again the problem of significant differences was discussed and the concept of chi square introduced. They were then taught how to use a nomograph for determining the significance of the difference between percentages.

LESSON FIVE: An Experience in Experimental Research

To provide an experience in experimental research and to develop an understanding of additional research concepts, the High Achievers served as subjects of an experiment on the effects of differential rewards upon various kinds of creative thinking. The general hypothesis upon which the experiment was based is that pupils tend to achieve along whatever lines they are rewarded.

Procedure

The two classrooms were each divided randomly into Groups A and B. This was done by having each pupil draw an assignment card from a stack which had been carefully and obviously shuffled. The two experimenters tossed a coin to see who would have which group and who would handle which treatment. (These arrangements were made rather obvious to communicate the concepts of randomization of treatments and the like. Afterwards the reasons for them were explained.) All A's assembled in one room and all B's in the other.

Group A was given the following instructions:

Your task is to think of ideas for improving this stuffed toy dog so that it will be more fun for a child to play with. Try to think of as many ideas as you can. Don't worry about how good your ideas are or how much it would cost to carry them out. A prize of two dollars will be awarded to the one who thinks of the largest number of ideas, regardless of how clever or original they are. Of course you want to think of clever and original ideas, so we shall give a prize of twenty-five cents to the one who thinks of the largest number of unusual or original ideas. You will have only ten minutes, so you will want to make good use of your time.

Group B was shown identically the same stuffed toy dog and given essentially the same instructions, except that the rewards for originality and fluency were reversed.

Responses were scored for fluency, flexibility, and originality. Fluency was determined by counting the number of relevant ideas given. Ideas not related to the improvement of the toy as something to play with were eliminated. Flexibility was determined by counting the number of different approaches used in making the improvements. A response was scored as original if it were given by fewer than 5 per cent of the subjects in a norm population of 600 subjects and if it showed creative strength (were not obvious).

Reporting Results

The results of the experiment were reported to the class on the following day, as shown in Table 1.

TABLE 1

Means, Standard Deviations, and Tests of Significance of Differences of Mean Fluency, Flexibility, and Originality Scores under Two Conditions

Score and Condition	Number	Mean	Standard Deviation	t-Ratio	Probability
Fluency, condition A	23	23.0	7.95		
Fluency, condition B	22	20.4	6.73	1.19	<.25
Flexibility, condition A	23	8.5	2.43		
Flexibility, condition B	22	8.5	1.84	0.00	—
Originality, condition A	23	6.2	3.60		
Originality, condition B	22	12.2	6.12	4.00	<.001

These results provided an excellent opportunity to illustrate the concept of level of confidence, since each of the three results can be accepted at different levels of confidence. The difference in originality can be accepted with a high level of confidence. We can have little confidence in the difference in fluency, and there is no difference at all in flexibility. The results suggest that rewarding originality in thinking does in fact increase the originality of the ideas produced without greatly affecting the number of ideas produced.

The results also provide data for showing that some experimental treatments produce greater variability or are more erratic in their effects than others. Under the conditions of the present experiment rewarding originality produces greater variability in originality scores than does rewarding fluency. (The difference is statistically significant at the 5 per cent level of confidence.)

The results were presented to the class in graphic form also, both to communicate the results more effectively and to give the class another model for use in presenting data.

LESSON SIX:
An Experiment of Their Own

The climax of the course was an experiment conducted by the High Achievers themselves in the third, fourth, and fifth grades. Experience had shown that it was not desirable to have them conduct experiments in the other sixth grade classes.

The Pilot Study

To give the students experience in dealing with the materials of the experiment, a pilot study was conducted with the High Achievers as subjects. They were given the following Horse-Trading Problem:

You bought a horse for $60 and sold it for $70. You then decided that you wanted the horse back. You had to pay $80 for it this time but you sold it again for $90. How did you come out in all of this trading? Did you make or lose any money? How much did you gain or lose, if any?

When asked for their responses, the following results were obtained:

- 19 said that he would gain $10.
- 14 said that he would break even.
- 6 said that he would make $20.

No one said that he would gain $30, until the experimenter asked those who had not held up their hands if they had gotten $30 (the least frequent incorrect answer in most groups tested by the first author). After the correct answer ($20) had been given and discussed, it was noted that some of them were uncertain of their answer and were willing to shift to an incorrect answer.

The High Achievers were then given the instructions for conducting the experiment. The class was divided into ten research teams, given the materials they would need to conduct the experiment (step-by-step procedures for experiment, answer cards, and retest questionnaires), and assigned classrooms for the conduct of the experiment the following morning. On the following day they were given some more tools for analyzing their data to describe and draw inferences concerning the problem being studied. They were given practice in converting proportions to per cents, using the nomograph to determine the level of confidence of differences in per cents, making bar graphs, and the like. They were also given the following dittoed outline to guide them in preparing their reports:

One important aspect of the research process is the communication of your results to others. When we find out something, we want to tell others about it. A good research report should tell the following five things:

1. **THE PURPOSE OF THE STUDY:** Why did you perform the study? What was it that you didn't know? What were you trying to find out?

2. **PROCEDURES:** What was done? Who performed the experiment? What materials did they use? Who were the subjects? How many were there? What did the experimenter do and what did the subjects do? These things should be described in such a way that someone else could carry out the study and expect to obtain the same results.

3. **RESULTS:** What happened? What did you find out? This should include a presentation of your data in tables, charts, or the like.

4. **DISCUSSION:** What do your results mean? Try to explain your findings and their meaning.

5. **CONCLUSIONS:** What does it all add up to? What can you be reasonably certain about? How certain can you be?

The Reports

Each of the ten research teams brought its completed report to the last meeting of the class. Almost all of the reports were well-organized and were written in good form. It was evident from most of the reports that the writing had been a team effort, each making a contribution.

FINDINGS FROM THE TOTAL STUDY

One by-product of teaching gifted children research skills and concepts is the contribution experiments conducted in such settings make to the development and testing of new hypotheses. As already shown, the historical research project yielded a number of hypotheses which had not occurred previously to the first author. The experiment conducted by the children helped plot in a new way the increase in peer influence and the decline in adult influence in searching for solutions to problems.

No attempt was made to make a comprehensive evaluation of the outcomes of this one-week course on research. Three sets of evidence, however, provide at least a tentative evaluation of some of the outcomes of this set of experiences. A brief inventory test administered during the last twenty minutes of the course indicated that some of the High Achievers had mastered almost all of the concepts and that a majority of them had mastered all except five of the 43 concepts included in the test. Certain experiences during the week indicated that the teachers had modified the way in which they perceived some of their pupils' potentialities. Follow-up discussions with the principal, teachers, and pupils five months later indicated that many of the concepts and skills introduced were used throughout the remainder of the term in a variety of ways in all areas of the curriculum. Decades later, contacts between the first author and parents of the students indicate that the concepts and skills taught were used throughout the participants' educational and professional experiences.

CONCEPTS OF QUALITATIVE RESEARCH

Although the example used in this chapter focuses on quantitative research, teachers of gifted and talented and children in the regular classroom should be aware of the concepts and skills of qualitative research. Most of the research projects described by Renzulli and his associates (Renzulli, 1977, 1994; Renzulli, Reis, & Smith, 1981) make use of qualitative research concepts and skills.

In recent years there have been many developments concerning qualitative research (Mason, 1996; Simonton, 1990; Wallgren, Wallgren, & Persson, 1996) that have been made and have gained in popularity and respect. The historological research project described in this chapter combines quantitative and qualitative methods. Simonton's (1990) book on historiometry describes some advanced developments for making historigraphical research more objective. Interest in futurism or the study of the future has resulted in advances in qualitative methods. Hencley and Yates (1974) have described several applications.

Teachers of gifted and talented children in the regular classroom should give attention to graphing statistics and data. This can be used to make statistics and data more alive to all children in the regular classroom. Wallgren, Wallgren, Persson and Jorner (1996) provides a useful reference.

CONCLUSIONS

We believe that we and others have demonstrated that elementary school children can joyfully master research concepts and skills. We are fully aware that there is a reluctance to embrace these concepts even in gifted education because teachers are ill-trained or untrained in statistics and research methodology. In Japan where statistics and research methods are a part of the regular elementary school curriculum this fear does not exist. Children in the third, fourth, and fifth grades take research projects in stride. It is gratifying to observe that concepts and skills of both statistical and qualitative research are beginning to be used with gifted and talented children in the United States.

12

Motivation

I N *Composing a Life*, Mary Catherine Bateson (1989) describes life as a work in progress and calls this process an act of creation. She views everyone as being engaged in the act of creation — creating a composition of their lives. Reflecting on this concept, it is apparent that each of us faces discontinuity, interruptions and conflicted priorities, yet if these are viewed as a source of wisdom and as a vital part of life, then our energies can be narrowed to focus, define and assist us in becoming achievers. The major question for this chapter is how can teachers best help gifted students to understand and to believe that they are able to take charge of life circumstances and become highly motivated achievers.

Torrance (1965a) defines motivation as involving all the variables that arouse, sustain and direct behavior. This means that a gifted student lacking motivation is not sufficiently aroused and sustained to learn anything near the level of which he or she is capable. Educators are beginning to recognize that in school, learning the basics is not enough, and if today's students are to take charge of their destiny, they need to learn to set goals and to know how and when to seek assistance for reaching their goals. One method of motivating students that the authors have found very helpful is engaging the students in as much of the classroom management as possible whether it involves the selection of materials, teaching strategies for the classroom, formulating ways to study the materials or in evaluating the worthiness and appropriateness of the learning.

DEVELOPING HIGHLY MOTIVATED ACHIEVERS

For three years, June Maker, Roberta Daniels and Dorothy Sisk focused on developing underachieving students into highly motivated achievers. In Project Step Up (Systematic Training for Educational Programs for

Underserved Pupils), a research and teacher training project funded by the U.S. Department of Education Javits program, the three teacher trainers worked with 216 high potential minority economically disadvantaged children in the states of Arizona, Arkansas, Florida and Texas (Sisk, 1993). Project Step Up administered pre and post test with continuous assessment of the students to identify their educational benchmarks and learning levels. Once these benchmarks in reading, mathematics and writing were identified, then the Project staff assisted the staff teachers in developing appropriate lessons at each student's level of learning to help insure opportunities for success in the classroom. The Structure of Intellect (SOI) battery was administered as a pre- and post-test measure indicate to chart the individual student's growth in processing and diagnostic abilities. The SOI indicates each child's processing strengths and areas that need to be developed. The primary Step Up objective was to empower the individual students, and to accomplish this objective, the teachers were asked to explain the purpose of each lesson and learning activity to their students, so that they could in turn articulate the purpose of the learning and truly feel "engaged" in the learning process.

A key principle of Step Up was the creation of a positive and responsive classroom atmosphere. When visitors observe Step Up classes, they consistently note the high energy and receptive environment of the teachers, students and parents — all learning together. The project has continued with local school districts supporting the project. Currently there are twelve active sites.

Each summer, a one week training institute is held for parents and teachers at Lamar University in Beaumont, Texas for the Project Step Up participants. In the summer of 1996, fifty teachers and parents attended, and in daily seminars, they concentrated on a variety of engaging teaching strategies including futures (Sisk & Whaley, 1987), leadership (Sisk & Rosselli, (1987), and intuitive thinking (Shallcross & Sisk, 1989) to motivate themselves and their students. One of the major factors that we discovered in the seminars that contributes to low motivation of both students and teachers is the lack of dreams or goals, and an overwhelming sense that individual goals are not attainable.

By the second grade, where Project Step Up was initiated, most of the children have already internalized the low expectations that significant adults (both parents and teachers) hold for them. The children and their parents report that they are full of negative feelings and attitudes about school. Many of the parents state that school was not a happy place for them and that their subsequent lack of commitment to work on a GED, Family Literacy or in ESL (English as a Second Language) programs stems from their basic belief that no one really cares about them or their education.

As a result of this feedback, one of the major challenges that we address in Project Step Up is how to provide the students and their parents with the necessary skills and strategies to become successful learners and how to build a strong sense of community in which the parents, teachers and students can experience working together on common goals. To meet this challenge in the classroom, the teachers share classroom responsibility with their students, encouraging them to monitor their own learning programs. They use numerous wall charts and individual portfolios to portray visually the students' goals and progress. The classroom walls display student products, work charts list a variety of words (descriptive, action), samples of ideas about current topics and learning models such as Calvin Taylor's Creative Talents, (1964) and Howard Gardner's Multiple Intelligences Model (1983). These visual representations serve as constant encouragement to the children to think and to reflect on their learning processes. The students are also provided multiple choices of activities, learning products and learning preferences.

In Project Step Up, the 3 C's of caring, community and choice are stressed. Students engage in small group work for specific skill development or work on individual or group research. The children begin spontaneously to learn when to group and regroup themselves on need.

Computers are a vital part of Project Step Up's effort to build specific skills, and the students are required to write and read in both their primary language and second language. Each classroom is equipped with at least six computers purchased by Title I funds and Javits grant funds. In Arizona, the Step Up students are primarily Navajo; in Texas and Florida, they are primarily Hispanic and African-American, and in Arkansas, African-American.

GUIDELINES FOR ESTABLISHING HIGH MOTIVATIONAL CLASSROOMS

The following guidelines were found to be effective by Step Up Teachers:

- Use task appropriate lessons for individual students.
- Use positive language and behavior.
- Use classroom time for daily goal setting and planning long term projects.
- Use choice and individual decision-making to establish shared control.
- Use a focused learning approach for skill development.
- Use classroom meetings for discussions and celebrations of individual and group accomplishments to promote a sense of positive growth and to build a valuing of one another's progress. Classroom meetings also serve to stimulate a sense of anticipation of future learning.

Since the majority of Step Up students are bilingual, we focus on building cultural bridges from the specific Navajo, Hispanic and African-

American culture to the Anglo culture. In addition, we work on building personal ownership of the project in the local schools and stress that parents, teachers and students work as a team.

A sense of personal power and motivation is encouraged by

- Developing the students' sense of worth
- Developing a sense of individual high potentiality with mentors and role models
- Involving the families in establishing learning goals and shaping the ongoing design process of the program
- Focusing on the development of the perspective that teachers, administrators and parents care about children's success
- Resisting negative experiences, stereotypes or behaviors that imply children, parents or teachers are in any manner not worthy.

Project Step Up is a highly successful program. After the initial three years (1990-93), 50% of the participating children were able to qualify for their district's gifted program. The students identified in the project are represented in Figure 12.1. This accomplishment is remarkable in that at the onset of the project, none of the participating children could either qualify for the gifted program nor would they have been referred by their teachers as potential candidates. At the beginning of the project, most of the students were underachieving, many scoring well below the 50 percentile on group achievement and ability test scores.

Figure 12.1. Students identified as gifted at end of project (solid area).

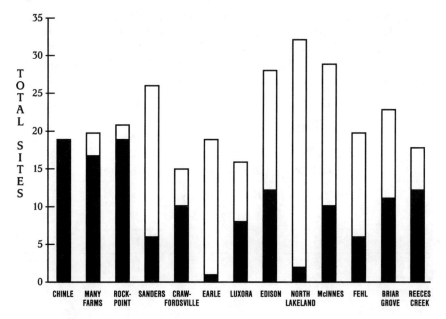

Table 12.1. Standardized pre and post test data: OLSAT (Otis Lennon Standard Achievement Test), DCAT (Developmental Cognitive Ability Test) for Reeces Creek Elementary, Killeen, Texas.

ID	OLSAT (Otis-Lennon)	OLSAT (Otis-Lennon)	OLSAT (Otis-Lennon)	DCAT (Spatial)
	Pre-test: 1991	Post-test: 1992	Gain	%
1	109	116	+ 7	87-S
2	126	141	+15	93-S
3	100	110	+10	82-S
4	114	119	+ 5	83-S
5	106	119	+13	87-S
6	109	120	+11	87-S

The test data from one of our project sites in Reeces Creek Elementary School in Houston, Texas, indicates the significant increase in pre- and post-test scores of the children on the Otis Lennon Standard Achievement Test (OLSAT). We also administered the Developmental Cognitive Abilities Test (DCAT), and many of the students achieved above the 85% in the spatial component of the test. The Fort Bend school district used the subtest scores on the DCAT as test data for considering the children's placement in the gifted program.

At a second site, Fehl Elementary School in Beaumont, Texas, students were given pre- and post-tests on the OLSAT, and the TONI (Test of Non-verbal Intelligence) was administered to verify the gain. For example, a student achieved 108 on a pre-test OLSAT and 118 on the post-test, 94% on the California Test of Basic Skills (CTBS) and 135 on the TONI and was enrolled in the gifted program.

Table 12.2. Standardized pre and post test data: OLSAT, CTBS, TONI for Fehl Elementary, Beaumont, Texas.

ID	OLSAT (Otis-Lennon)	OLSAT (Otis-Lennon)	OLSAT (Otis-Lennon)	TONI
	Pre-test: 1991	Post-test: 1992	Gain	IQ
1	106	127	+21	120
2	105	119	+14	120
3	108	118	+10	135
4	101	120	+19	130

GUIDING PRINCIPLES OF THE STEP UP PROGRAM INCLUDE:

- Provide appropriate instructional strategies and level of performance
- Establish individual classes of eighteen to twenty students working with teachers who either travel with their children from grades 2, 3 and 4 or work closely with the new teachers
- Articulate the program purpose clearly to build a sense of high motivation in teachers, parents and students and to raise student achievement and ability levels
- Provide a comprehensive program that works with parents, teachers, students and community
- Be responsive to the differing values, concerns, and behavioral manifestations of the talents and abilities of all participating ethnic and cultural groups.

In summary, Torrance's (1965a) statements of the most important reasons why gifted children are so poorly motivated continue to be true in the 90's.

- No Chance To Use What is Learned
- Interest In What Is Learned Rather Than Grades
- Learning Tasks Too Difficulty or Too Easy
- No Chance To Use Best Abilities
- No Chance To Learn in Preferred Ways
- Learning Lacking in Purposefulness

We would like to share information from a Project Step Up case study, that of Marisol, a 10 year old Hispanic girl who participated in the program for three years in Houston, Texas. In a recent visit to her classroom she said, "I don't know who thought up this Step Up program, but I want you to know that it has changed my life. I know what I want to be, a Doctor and I will be a good one." Applying the Bateson (1989) concept, Marisol is in the act of creation: composing her dream, her life, and she is focused and motivated to achieve that life goal.

IMPORTANT STEP UP PRINCIPLES TO BUILD MOTIVATION

To build motivation in children, we found that it is essential that teachers serve as facilitators. A facilitating teacher will:

- Focus on students' emotional, social and cognitive development

- Match curriculum to student learning levels and interests
- Integrate learning across subject areas
- Introduce higher level thinking skills, reinforce and demonstrate the use of the skills in all subject areas
- Emphasize higher level questioning processes
- Provide mentorships and role models
- Develop thematic units in all content areas
- Emphasize language arts integrated with arts

CONCLUSION

We would like to close this chapter on motivation with a poem written by our colleague George Betts (1995), who captures the importance of motivation.

> Some people have the ability
> to create excitement in their lives
>
> They are the ones who strive,
> who grow,
> who give and share,
> They are the ones who love . . .
>
> They possess passion . . .
> for themselves, others,
> Nature and experiences.
>
> They have the ability
> to see beyond today,
> to rise above the hectic pace,
> to strive for their own perfection . . .
>
> And they are gentle,
> for they love themselves,
> and they love others . . .
> Through their living
> they create peace and contentment.
>
> At the same time
> they create excitement,
> for there is always another mountain,
> a deeper joy,
> a new dawn . . .

13

Mentoring

A T SEVERAL POINTS in this book, the authors have pointed out that not all the needs of gifted and talented children can be met in the classroom. The authors have also described and discussed several devices that may be used to take gifted and talented children beyond the classroom. In Chapter 11, for example, the authors discussed the matter of doing research, which is a very powerful means of going beyond the classroom. In earlier chapters we have also described creative problem solving, creative reading, and the incubation model of teaching. For example, the incubation model frequently takes children beyond the classroom — interviewing experts, reading from other sources, experimentation, and other ways of finding out.

The authors have long stressed the importance of falling in love with something — a dream, an image of the future. We are convinced that the driving force behind future achievements is having an image of the future. These images draw us on, energize us, give us the courage and will to take important initiatives to move forward to new solutions and creative achievements. To dream and to plan, to be curious about the future, and to wonder how it can be influenced by our efforts are an important part of our being human.

Many of the gifted and talented children who participated in one of the first author's (Torrance, 1981) longitudinal studies of creative achievement told of their falling in love with something while they were in elementary school and how it had influenced their adult creative achievement. A few examples will be given to illustrate. Mack began making science fiction drawings in the second grade, and in the third grade he was writing science fiction stories and space dramas that his classmates enacted. He was also gifted in music, art, and science. While in high school, he organized the Minnesota Science Fiction Society which continued to publish a science fiction magazine long afterwards. His list of awards include creative musical and acting performances, musical compositions, business entrepreneurships, and a career as a forecaster in business and now in the State Department. He has also published science fiction.

Robert, one of Mack's classmates, fell in love with inventing in the third grade and kept the classroom cluttered with his inventions, just as Mack kept things covered with his space age drawings. Robert has a Ph. D. degree in engineering and was still inventing with a corporation in the forefront of his field. At the time he completed his follow up questionnaire, his aspiration was to become an independent inventor. This would free him to "play his own game in his own way" to a greater degree. A couple of months after he had returned his questionnaire, he had an inventive breakthrough that he believes will make him an independent inventor.

All of the young people in this longitudinal study have exciting stories to tell of their search for identity and their struggle to find ways of "playing their game" and doing the thing that they are in love with. Some of their stories are heartbreaking, yet we can learn important lessons from them. Many of them have their dreams and respect the things that they were in love with. Teachers, parents, and mentors helped them learn how to "play their own games," and this has made a difference in their lives and in their achievements. This enabled them to pursue the thing that they are in love with and make useful social contributions.

This love of something must somehow be fueled by experiences outside the classroom. Having a mentor can be a key factor in the search.

INTRODUCTION

At the 1990 educational summit in Charlottesville, Virginia, President George Bush and the Governors of the United States established the National Goals for Education calling for a renaissance in education and the placement of high values on the National Goals that recommended sweeping fundamental changes in the American educational system. They also recommended that education be given more flexibility to devise challenging and inspiring strategies to meet the needs of an ever increasing diverse population of students.

Former Secretary of Labor, Elizabeth Dole (1989) described the American workplace as being in a state of unreadiness, unready for new realities and particularly unready for the challenge of the 90's. Dole (1989) states that the connection between educational excellence and business success is fundamental. Closer ties between education and business must be formed.

Mentoring programs meet the recommendations of Dole and the National Goals for Education. Mentorship programs offer considerable flexibility because they can be arranged beyond the time, location and method constraints of traditional education. When mentoring programs are offered to students, they help unite education, business, government and the private sector. When mentors and students interact one-on-one, they create a means to integrate the necessary knowledge, skills and abilities needed by the students.

The gains for students and mentors have been documented extensively. Boston (1976); Runions (1980); and Torrance (1984) have explored the meaning of mentoring as they have defined the roles of a mentor and mentee for gifted students. The benefits have been documented by Cox and Daniel (1983); Cox, Daniel and Boston (1985); Feldhusen (1989); Lambert & Lambert (1982); Seeley (1985); Shapiro (1988); and Sisk (1987).

CLASSIC MODEL OF MENTORSHIP

Hirsch developed a model for the development of mentorship programs with support and funding from the U. S. Office of Gifted and Talented in 1976-79. Hirsch (1979) worked primarily with secondary students who received one semester of credit for high school and were assigned to mentors or community leaders in decision-making positions. The students also attended weekly seminars in which their teachers employed the Harvard case study method to encourage them to share experiences, insights, and problems.

The comments of two students involved in a mentorship program based on the Hirsch model indicate the high degree of success (Sisk, (1987).

Stephanie: As long as I can remember I've always wanted to be a lawyer, so that's why I enjoy my mentorship with a court reporter. My observation of the day to day involvement with Ms. Paul is exciting, and there isn't a day that goes by that I don't thoroughly enjoy seeing the human action of life. I know I will be a much better lawyer as a result of this experience. I am certainly learning a lot about efficient use of time and the importance of scheduling.

An interesting and important factor to consider when reading Stephanie's comments is that she is an underachieving African American student from a low income family. Through the mentor intervention, her absenteeism was drastically reduced and her school achievement improved.

Another example of a successful mentorship is that of Robert.

Robert: I've always been a ham and interested in acting, but I just didn't think I could make it. But since I've been at the Inner City Theater with Mr. Jones, I feel it is not only a possibility for me, but I am going to do it, I can act. I have had several parts and Mr. Jones has helped me believe in myself. I know when I am reaching the audiences and when I am not. There is a feeling of realness that goes through me when I am on the stage, and it is wonderful . . . so wonderful I can hardly explain it to anyone but Mr. Jones. He listens and never becomes angry with me when I forget a line. If my other teachers were like he is, I wouldn't have wasted as much time in school.

At one time there were over fifty mentorship programs throughout the United States known as Executive Intern Programs. One state that implemented the Hirsch model on a state wide basis was Florida. During the 1980-90 period, there were ten school districts in Florida with over 300 secondary student participants. Another state that is very successful in implementing mentor programs is Minnesota. In the twin cities region of Minnesota, the Mentor Connection program has successfully allowed hundreds of high school students to prepare for and participate in advanced level learning with mentors in their fields of interest.

In spite of the fact that most mentor programs have been planned for secondary students, there is no reason that mentor programs cannot be made available to elementary students. Using the classical definition of mentor, an individual with expertise sharing experience with another, a mentor could be an older student sharing experiences with another younger student, as well as adults from the community/business sector. One neglected source of mentors is the retiree. Many retirees have considerable leadership experience, knowledge and the time to devote to gifted students.

Mentorship programs have been presented in such a manner that the typical teacher or administrator does not see the development of mentor programs as practical or as one teacher stated as "doable." Mentor programs are much more than asking someone in the workplace to mentor a gifted student. They involve orientation, training and follow-up for both the mentor and the student. Time is an important element as well as appropriate funding, and, most important, encouragement is needed for the staff who develop the mentor program.

IDENTIFYING STUDENTS FOR MENTORSHIPS

In identifying students who may need and or merit a mentorship, one of the first questions to ask is does the student need additional enrichment? If so, are there specific topics or subject areas that the student wants to know or learn about? How much time and energy can the student devote to a mentorship? Are the parents willing to assist the student in seeking out new opportunities? Can the parent provide transportation, supplies, space? If not, do the parents know someone who might provide the resources?

Before deciding on the use of a mentor from the outside of your school district, it is helpful to see if any specialist within the school or school system can help the student or an older student with expertise in the topic area may also be enlisted.

It is also helpful to start a portfolio for the student that includes experiences that the student has already accomplished, extra courses, clubs, outside reading, independent research and work experiences. Once the topic is identified that the student wants to explore, then the teacher can assist the student to brainstorm possible activities and resources that might provide independent study opportunities. Consider available community education classes, wildlife centers and public park programs.

The teacher or administrator in charge of the mentorship program may want to ask a specialist to come and visit with the classroom in which the potential mentee is enrolled. In this way, the specialist would be able to offer enrichment to all students while directly working with the one student who is interested in the mentorship. If the students' interest, drive and enthusiasm are sufficient, you may want to arrange for the student to visit with a specialist in the workplace and observe or begin a "shadowing" experience.

After the meeting and shadowing, the mentorship or internship can be arranged between the student and the expert. This can be done during school time as in the Executive Intern program in St. Petersburg, Florida, during the summer or during release time from school.

All of the above procedures take time, but the time is well worth the effort and commitment. The director of the St. Petersburg, Florida program reports that it might take a period of months or even years to identify the right specialist. One of the major payoffs for school districts that decide to use mentorships is that it brings parents, students, schools and the community together in a very positive manner.

CHARACTERISTICS OF GIFTED MENTEES

Beard and Densen (1986) report that the profiles of mentees who attend the Learning Activity Mentor Program (LAMP) in New Zealand are very able, divergent students who lack high esteem. This last characteristic is atypical for most mentor programs in the United States. Most programs describe their students as having high self esteem. However, the highly individualized nature of mentorships allows each student to experience activities tailored to each student's needs and can address the special needs of low esteem students, good communicators, intellectually and socially mature, committed to their area of interest, hardworking, highly motivated, organized planners, and above all curious.

Reilly (1992) lists the following student characteristics for consideration for a mentorship:
- Motivated by challenges
- Creative
- Willing to work hard
- Looking for advanced learning
- Able to provide your own transportation

- Willing to minimize outside of school work hours
- Willing to complete an application
- Acceptable to a screening committee
- Willing to complete a meaningful learning project

ADVANTAGES OF MENTORSHIPS

In talking with one of the mentor program directors in Florida, she quickly listed several advantages that included hands on learning, strengthening interpersonal skills, advanced learning and knowledge, access to experts in a given field, one on one personal learning and involvement in a meaningful research project. The objectives of her mentorship program were (1) to provide students opportunities to learn beyond the limits of time, space and curriculum, (2) to provide students access to resources and facilities not usually available in schools, (3) to provide students with professional role models and (4) to stimulate career awareness and career options.

ARE MENTORS HARD TO IDENTIFY?

One of the first questions that educators ask who are considering developing mentor programs is, How hard is it to identify mentors? Interestingly enough, most experts are willing to be mentors. They like sharing responsibilities, and they are dedicated to the notion of developing new talent for their profession. Several mentors that we interviewed indicated that being a mentor was one way of giving back the help that they had received, and others indicated that they were mentors because they had not been able to experience a mentorship.

SELECTING MENTORS

Most mentor programs report that they have steering teams to help select mentors. Interested co-workers can be surveyed for possible mentors. Parents can be asked to provide names of mentors, and school volunteer programs are an excellent resource bank. Chambers of Commerce, community education, colleges and universities, service organizations, clubs, and voluntary action centers are also useful resources. In addition, the Yellow Pages and local newspapers and magazines can be a source of potential names.

The names that are compiled represent a resource file that can be updated on a regular basis. The mentor team can be asked to interview the mentors. It is also important that the mentors have enough time to help students carry out a project. Another important consideration is student safety. In addition, the subject or technical expertise of the mentor needs to be verified. This can be done by merely asking questions concerning the potential mentor's business, position and education or training.

A very important consideration for choosing mentors is the communication skill that the mentors use in dealing with young people and are they enthusiastic and committed to being mentors?

Haeger and Feldhusen (1989) suggest aspects to look for in a mentor who will work with gifted adolescents and so does Flaxman, Asher and Harrington (1988). Gray (1988) reports on spontaneous mentorships and Reilly (1992) suggests the following considerations:

- Is the prospective mentor flexible?
- Does the mentor have good people skills; people oriented and enthusiastic?
- Is he/she comfortable with teenagers?
- Is he/she sensitive to student needs and in setting expectations for them?
- Can the mentor generate new questions or research for the student to pursue?
- Is he/she willing and able to help identify potential problems and find solutions for them?
- Can the mentor provide constructive evaluation and feedback to nurture the student's growth?
- Does he/she perceive possible benefits to the student, business, community, and most important for himself/herself?

MONITORING MENTORSHIP PROGRAMS

One simple way of monitoring a mentorship program is keeping attendance records. Another means is the use of class discussions or a seminar that is a required part of the mentorship program. Most mentorship programs report that they require weekly reports from the mentees as well as attendance at the weekly seminars. We also recommend that a visit to the mentor site be made which can include a guided tour of the site, a brief chat with the mentor concerning the student's progress, and observation of the student at work.

Still another important part of evaluation is the recognition of the work of mentors, students and the staff in the mentorship program, particularly the steering committee. Some programs report that they have a recognition luncheon; others hold annual dinners and or open houses. At these recognition and evaluation sessions, it is important to provide time for the mentors and mentees to share their experiences. As they share their advanced learning and sense of pride in their mentor-mentee relations, they build added commitment to the experience.

MENTOR RELATIONSHIPS

In considering the nature of mentor relationships, it must be recognized that mentors need to continue to fulfill other responsibilities while assuming this role. Mentors serve as a channel for information and wisdom from other sources. They also provide structure, express positive expectations, serve as advocates, share themselves, and make the experience special (Noller & Frey, 1995). Mentors are often able to see potential that has not been realized by the students and can help them to become aware of this potential and to develop it.

A mentor relationship in which there is an emphasis on recognizing and developing talents involves three critical elements, according to Noller and Frey (1995, pp. 205-206).

Firgure 13.1. A Mentoring Relationship

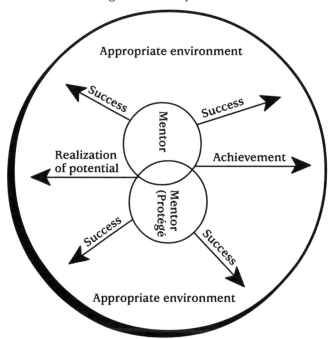

"It must first present an arena within which goal oriented activity can occur. This environment is usually provided by an organization, such as a school district, a program sponsor or other interested parties. It is a setting for problem solving, providing for interaction between the mentor and the mentee (protégé). The mentor and the mentee, of course, are the other two critical elements. Success is predicated on a mutually compatible relationship focused upon clearly defined objectives. The specific interactions are unique to each situation. These three factors, and their interaction, are depicted in Figure 13.1.

Many programs use written reports that the mentor and mentee complete. Areas included on a number of evaluation forms include questions that address self awareness, career and college planning, research ability, interpersonal communication, and valuing of cultural diversity.

Mentoring relationships affect and benefit gifted and talented students, as well as the faculty and schools that are involved. Reilly (1992) reports that the students receive advanced thinking skills in their chosen field, more clearly defined career options, connections between work and school, increased motivation to achieve, friendships with mentors and fellow students, inspiration generated by a role model, a matured sense of responsibility and direction, and better understanding and development of their potential. The potential effect on the staff according to most programs is an increased sense of professionalism, pride in the student's accomplishment and renewed interest in their field. School districts also benefit in the increased number of energized students and staff.

Mentors that we interviewed report that they feel they learn more than the student, experience greater pride in their field, feel a sense of satisfaction, and establish lasting friendships with their mentee.

A variety of good resources exist regarding mentoring gifted and talented children. Torrance (1984) has presented statistical data from his 22-year longitudinal study to show that having a mentor does aid creative achievement. He also describes how mentor relationships endure, change, and die. Nash and Treffinger (1993) present a step-by-step guide for creating an effective mentor program in schools. Goff and Torrance (1991) have compiled a guide for mentors and mentees. Reilly (1992) has written about the mentorship concept and presents an essential guide for mentoring in both school and business. Torrance, Goff, and Satterfield (1996) have dealt interestingly about the special problems of mentoring in the culture of poverty. They describe how children who are living in poverty, failing in school, engaging in delinquent behavior, and are unmotivated are helped through a mentor to become motivated and become high achievers.

Being a mentor in the culture of poverty makes heavy demands upon the mentor. It requires more time, patience, creative problem solving, and probably money. There are, however, several resources of such mentors, including retired teachers of children coming from the culture of poverty, retired people in general, clubs or organizations dedicated to this purpose, and certain civic organizations. Mentors in the culture of poverty have to find opportunities otherwise denied their mentees.

Of all the groups who come from the culture of poverty, greatest concern has been expressed about black boys. Their dropout rate, violence, robbery, rape, and other juvenile crimes are alarming. One organization that is successfully combatting this problem is the 100 Black Men's Club through its mentoring program for black boys. One such mentor is an Athens, Georgia, black judge. His mentee is a 10-year old black boy who has never known a father. Hoping to fire up his mentee's interest in politics, the judge and his mentee worked on a diagram of the federal, state, and local government. In the process, the judge worked in a few lessons about life in general.

The mentee says that he wants to be a lawyer one day and he has already spent some time in court observing his mentor. The mentee said, "We have lots of fun, and we go to a lot of places. He's my friend, and he's like a father I never had." The judge said he has seen the positive results that another supportive adult in a child's life can have. As a judge, he has seen some harsh results the lack of such a relationship can bring. He cites the time he had to sentence a 16-year old to a lengthy prison sentence for robbery. He said, "I honestly think that if he had a mentor of some type that would not have happened. . . . I think being a mentor is the most effective way to help kids. It's one on one."

Other mentors in this program include a deputy sheriff, a policeman, business men, a lawyer, and the like.

There are a number of other vehicles that are being used to mobilize resources outside the classroom to meet the needs of gifted and talented children and adolescents. Some of these are identified and described in Appendix D.

CONCLUSION

Mentoring is one of the prime devices for meeting the needs of gifted and talented children beyond the classroom. The value of mentoring in the adult achievement of gifted and talented children has been reported in Torrance's longitudinal study. The model of the mentoring process was described and illustrated by examples. Suggestions have been given for recruiting and assigning mentors and for monitoring mentorship programs. Attempts have been made to show how participating in a mentor program encourages students, teachers, mentors and parents to join hands to forge a nurturing relationship between the mentor and mentee and between the family and the school.

14

Becoming A Teacher Of Gifted And Talented Children

ONE'S TEACHING A UNIQUE INVENTION

THE PROCESS of becoming a teacher of gifted and talented children is much like the process of creative thinking itself. If you are counting upon your college education, your courses in education, your student teaching or this book to "make" you a teacher, you will be disappointed. You might learn much about the subjects you will be teaching, the nature of children, the learning process, the methods and materials of instruction, and the like, but this is not enough. In this book an effort has been made to acquaint you with the most forward-looking information available concerning the nature of giftedness and talent, the goals of educating gifted and talented children, ways of identifying and motivating them, and examples of how you can help them establish a sound foundation for continued development, develop as creative readers, and acquire some of the concepts and skills of investigation. All of these things are inadequate. They must be combined with your own potentialities and the needs of your own pupils in such a way as to become your own unique invention, your way of teaching. This unique invention of the teacher is tremendously important in the teaching of gifted and talented children to help them discover and become their potentialities.

The teacher's invention emerges through the creative process of trying to accomplish some goal. As you fail or succeed in your teaching goals, you become aware of your deficiencies, defects in your techniques and strategies, and gaps in your knowledge. You draw upon your past experiences and increase your search for clues in your ongoing experiences. You try to apply creatively the scientifically developed principles learned in your professional education or through your reading. Then you read and study and puzzle some more. You see things of which you have hitherto been unaware. You make guesses, or formulate hypotheses, concerning the solution. You test and modify these hypotheses and tell others what you have discovered. Through the pain and ecstasy that accompany this process, your personal invention occurs!

Since your way of teaching must be your own invention, no one can present you with a prescription for creating the conditions most favorable for the release of creativity. Your own personality, resources and needs, your intellectual resources and skills, the needs and abilities of your students, and the expectations of the community in which you are teaching all interact to determine the most effective methods and materials. It *is* possible, however, to derive from experience and research some general principles which increase markedly the chance that your teaching will release the potential of gifted and talented children and all children. It is possible to create teaching methods and instructional materials that have built into them many tested principles. It is the teacher's creative task to weave all of them into new combinations that meet the needs and abilities of the students and are in harmony with the needs and abilities of the teacher.

MAJOR REQUIREMENTS
OF THE TEACHER'S INVENTION

Frequently inventors and scientific discoverers have found their tasks easy as soon as they were able to define the characteristics or requirements of the invention or the object of their search. We can do this to a certain extent in regard to becoming a teacher of gifted and talented children. It seems rather certain in the light of the concepts of giftedness and talent presented in this book that teaching gifted children requires the most sensitive and alert kind of guidance and direction possible. It requires a most receptive type of listening, seeing, and feeling. The teacher of gifted and talented children should him/herself be fully alive, well educated, curious and excited about learning, and free of hostility and the pathological need to punish. He/she must be prepared to permit one thing to lead to another and in some cases to become the sponsor or mentor of gifted and creative children - or help them find someone else who can fill this role.

It is common for teachers to talk about the forces in their environment that inhibit them in realizing their potentialities as teachers. Certainly there are in our society and in our systems of education many forces that threaten the teacher's individuality and cause him/her to conform to behavioral norms. Let us take a look at some of the more common forces within ourselves that inhibit us in our search for our unique invention, our way of teaching.

RANDOM THINKING RATHER THAN ABSORBED THINKING

In achieving your unique invention, your way of teaching, there are times when you will need to give your mind completely to the problem. Some people incorrectly associate invention and discovery with a random, aimless kind of behavior. It is true that many great ideas seem to occur when a person is relaxed — while sitting in the bathtub, during church services, or while shaving. Unfailingly, however, such occurrences were preceded by periods of concentrated attention during which the mind had been wholly occupied with the problem.

NO TIME FOR THINKING AND DAYDREAMING

Absorbed thinking takes time. The clock is indeed a tyrant, but much can be done to soften its tyranny. One of the first things you have to do is get over the compulsion to look busy and decide to make thinking a legitimate activity. Do not be afraid to leave a part of your day unscheduled with activities in which you appear to be busy, do not be afraid to daydream occasionally, and do not be ashamed if someone catches you occasionally doing something in an absentminded manner.

LACK OF INTELLECTUAL HONESTY

We frequently fear being honest lest someone ridicule or denigrate our ideas. We have been conditioned in so many ways to be less than honest, narcoticizing our creative functioning. We desire to appear to be rather than really be. In achieving your unique way of teaching, you will want to free yourself of all encumbrances that hinder you in your work, all beliefs that are false, all conventions and forms that are cramping, and all duties other than those that help you and your pupils achieve your potentialities.

THE UNPREPARED MIND

Some people believe that the more you know, the less likely you are to produce inventions and discoveries. This is a false belief, however. "Chance favors the prepared mind," as Louis Pasteur said. However, we do encounter an interesting paradox on this point. Familiarity with existing knowledge is necessary for the achievement of new knowledge, yet the existence of prior knowledge about a problem hinders the possibilities of the achievement of new knowledge. Preconceptions are often blamed for missed discoveries. As pointed out in the chapter on creative reading, much depends upon the attitude you have toward the knowledge you possess.

FAILURE TO INVESTIGATE AND EXPLORE

Even studies of awareness and perception indicate that skills in these areas are dependent upon opportunities to investigate, explore, and examine the detailed nature of objects, situations, and ideas. In the life of the teacher of gifted and talented children there should never be any period when the process of experimentation and testing ceases.

FAILURE TO INVESTIGATE
THINGS ANEW AND IN DEPTH

Students in education frequently complain about repetition and emphasis on the commonplace and obvious. This is because they — and their teachers — have not mastered the skills of looking at things anew and in greater depth. From studies of perception, it is clear that the meaning and grasp of an object changes as you shift your point of observation. Details previously missed may become extremely important. After changing a goal or obtaining additional information, the meaning of something familiar may also change. Many inventions and discoveries (Gordon, 1961) occur through deliberate methods of making the familiar strange or unfamiliar.

IMPOVERISHED STORE OF IMAGERY

You will have difficulty in thinking creatively if you lack a rich store of imagery. A well-filled storehouse of imagery will be useful to the teacher of gifted children in search of his/her invention. One way of enriching your imagery is through developing a keen awareness of the environment by experiencing it in detail, by getting a variety of sensory experiences, through first-hand experiences, through empathizing and identifying with others, by becoming involved in life. Another way is through the world's literature.

FAILURE TO RECORD IDEAS

Sometimes you may feel rather devoid of ideas until you start recording them. We frequently fail to hold onto ideas because they occur at some of the funniest times and places and we fail to "capture" them. Even children can be motivated to cultivate the idea-trap habit of jotting down ideas for future use and developing them when the opportunity arises.

FEAR OF INDIVIDUALITY

It is difficult to free yourself from other people's "should's." We are so afraid that we are going to hurt someone's feelings or that someone is not going to like us that we make compromises which hurt both ourselves and others, reducing severely our potentialities. Very few truly creative people who have made outstanding contributions to society have been popular and well liked in their day. In fact, many of them have been hated. The truly creative person has something urgent to say and constantly seeks new aspects of the truth.

FAILURE TO BE ONESELF

Perhaps the most important word of counsel for the teacher of gifted children in becoming his/her potentialities as a teacher is that old truism, "Be yourself if you want to contribute anything original and worthwhile." Such advice is difficult to take because we are hampered by pretense and diffidence, self-doubts and lack of stable anchors, and confused self-concepts. Know the value of your intuitions, treat them tenderly, and cultivate the conditions that enable them to flourish.

CONCLUSION

The process of becoming a teacher of gifted and talented children has been characterized as a unique invention of the teacher. This process has been described. The major requirement of the teacher's invention have been identified and discussed. The obstacles that threaten this invention have been reviewed. The process of becoming a teacher of gifted and talented children is indeed an exciting and rewarding adventure.

References

Amabile, T. M. (1989). *Growing up creative: nurturing a lifetime of creativity*. Buffalo, NY: Creative Education Foundation Press.

Anderson, J. E. (1960). The nature of abilities. In E. P. Torrance (Ed.), *Talent and education*, pp. 9-13. Minneapolis: University of Minnesota Press.

Anderson, K. E. (Ed.) (1960). *Research on the academically talented student*. Washington, DC: National Education Association.

Applegate, M. (1962). *Easy in English*. Evanston, IL: Harper and Row.

Armstrong, T. (1993). *Seven kinds of smart; identifying and developing your many intelligences*. New York: Penguin.

Barron, F. (1957). Originality in personality and intellect. *Journal of Personality, 25*, 730-740.

Barron, F. (1990). *Creativity and psychological health*. Buffalo, NY: Creative Education Foundation Press.

Barron, F. (1995). *No rootless flower: an ecology of creativity*. Cresskill, NJ: Hampton Press.

Bateson, M. C. (1989). *Composing a life*. New York: Penguin.

Beard, E. M., & Denson, P. A. (1986). News around the world. *Mentoring International, 4*, 111-115.

Benzwie, T. (1995). *A moving experience*. Tucson, AZ: Zephyr Press.

Benzwie, T. (1996). *More moving experiences*. Tucson, AZ: Zephyr Press.

Betts, G. (1995). Encouraging lifelong learning through the autonomous learner's model in serving gifted and talented students. In J. Genshaft, J. M. Bireley, & C. Hollinger (Eds.), *Serving gifted and talented students*, pp. Austin, TX: Pro-Ed.

Binet, A. (1909). *Les idées modernes sur les enfants*. Paris: Flamarion.

Bloom, B. S. (1958). Some effects, social, and educational conditions on creativity. In C. W. Taylor (Ed.). *The second University of Utah research conference on the identification of creative scientific talent*, pp. 55-65. Salt Lake City: University of Utah Press.

Bloom, B. S. (1976). *Human characteristics and school learning*. New York: McGraw-Hill.

Boston, B. O. (1976). *The sorcerer's apprentice. A study of the role of the mentor*. Reston, VA: Council for Exceptional Children.

Brewer, C., & Campbell, D. G. (1991). *Rhythms of learning: creative tools of developing lifelong skills*. Tucson, AZ: Zephyr Press.

Bruner, J. S. (1960). *The process of education*. Cambridge, MA: Harvard University Press.

Burkhart, R. C. (1962). *Spontaneous and deliberate ways of learning*. Scranton, PA: International Textbook Co.

Burt, C. (1958). The inheritance of mental ability. *American Psychologist, 13*, 1-15.

Buzan, T. (1991). *Use both sides of your brain*. New York: Dutton.

Campbell, L., Campbell, B., & Dickinson, D. (1996). *Teaching and learning through multiple intelligences*. Tucson, AZ: Zephyr Press.

Ciardi, J. (1962). *I met a man*. Pathways of Sound.

Clymer, T. et al. (1969). *Reading 360 program*. Lexington, MA: Ginn & Co.

Clymer, T. et al. (1976). *Reading 720 program*. Lexington, MA: Ginn & Co.

Coffin, M. (1996). *Team science: organizing classrooms that develop group skills*. Tucson, AZ: Zephyr Press.

Corwin, R. B., & Friel, S. N. (1990). *Statistics: prediction and sampling. A unit of study from Used Numbers: Real Data in the Classroom*. Palo Alto, CA: Dale Seymour Publications.

Cox, J., & Daniels, N. (1983). The role of the mentor. *Gifted Children Today, 29*, 54-56.

Cox, J., Daniels, N., & Boston, B. O. (1985). *Educating able learners, programs and promising practices*. Austin, TX: University of Texas Press.

Crabbe, A. (1982). Creating a brighter future: an update on the future problem solving program. *Journal for the Education of the Gifted. 4*, 2-9.

Cunnington, B. F., Myers, R. E., Buckland, P., & Peterson, R. G. (1962). *Eyes at their fingertips*. Minneapolis, MN: Bureau of Educational Research, University of Minnesota.

Cunnington, B. F., & Torrance, E. P. (1965). *Giovanni and the giant*. Boston: Ginn.

Daurio, S. P. (1979). Education enrichment versus acceleration: a review of the literature. In W. C. George, S. J. Cohn, & J. C. Stanley (Ed.), *Educating the gifted: acceleration and enrichment*, pp. 13-63. Baltimore, MD: John Hopkins University Press.

Davis, G. A. (1983). *Creativity is forever* (2nd Ed.). Dubuque, IA: Kendall/Hunt.

de Bono, E. (1970). *Lateral thinking*. New York: Harper & Row.

de Bono, E. (1986). *de Bono's thinking course*. New York: Facts on File Publications.

de Groot, A. D. (1948). The effects of war upon the intelligence of youth. *Journal of Abnormal and Social Psychology, 43*, 311-317.

de Groot, A. D. (1951). War and intelligence of youth. *Journal of Abnormal and Social Psychology, 46*, 596-597.

DeHaan, R. F., & Havighurst, R. J. (1961). *Educating gifted children*. Chicago: University Press.

de Mille, R. (1973). *Put your mother on the ceiling*. New York: Viking.

Dewey, J. (1938). *Logic: the theory of inquiry*. New York: Henry Holt.

Dinkmeyer, D., & Dreikurs, R. (1963). *Encouraging children in learning*. Englewood Cliffs, NJ: Prentice-Hall.

Dole, E. (1989). State of the working place address. Washington, DC: Department of Labor.

Drews, E. M. (1961a). A critical evaluation of approaches to the identification of gifted students. In A. Traxler (Ed.), *Measurement and evaluation in today's schools*. pp. 47-51. Washington, DC: American Council on Education.

Drews, E. M. (1961b). Recent findings about gifted adolescents. In E. P. Torrance (Ed.). *New educational ideas: Third Minnesota Conference on gifted children*. pp. 26-49. Minneapolis: Center for Continuing Education, University of Minnesota.

Durrell, D. (February 24, 1961). Pupil team learning: effects of team size on retention of knowledge. Paper presented at Annual Meeting of the American Research Association, Chicago.

Durrell, D., & Chambers, J. R. (1958). Research in thinking abilities related to reading. *Reading Teacher, 12*, 89-91.

Ellet, P. (1993). Cooperative learning and gifted education. *Roeper Review, 16,* 114-116.

Feldhusen, H. (1993). *Individualized teaching of gifted children in regular classrooms.* West Lafayette, IN: Star Teaching Materials.

Feldhusen, J. (1989). Synthesis of research on gifted youth. *Educational Leadership, 46 (6)* 6-11.

Feldhusen, J. E., & Treffinger, D. (1985). *Creative thinking and problem solving and gifted education.* Dubuque, IA: Kendall/Hunt.

Ferebee, J. D. (1950). Learning through creative expression. *Elementary English, 27,* 73-78.

Ferguson, M. (1973). *The brain revolution: the frontiers of the mind.* New York: Taplinger Publishing Co.

Fine, R., Daly, D., & Fine, L. (1962). Psychodance and experiment and training. *Group Psychotherapy and Psychodrama, 15,* 2-3, 233.

Flaxman, E., Ascher, C., & Harrington, C. (1988). Youth mentoring: programs and practices. New York: ERIC Clearinghouse on Urban Education.

Fliegler, L. A. (1961). *Curriculum planning for the gifted.* Englewood Cliffs, NJ: Prentice-Hall.

Frankel, E. (1961). The gifted academic underachiever. *Science Teacher, 28,* 49-51.

Friel, S. N., Modros, J. R., & Russell, F. J. (1992). *Statistics: middles, means, and in-betweens. A unit of study for grades 5-6 from Used Numbers: Real Data in the Classroom.* Palo Alto, CA: Dale Seymour Publications.

Fritz, R. L. (August, 1958). An evaluation of scholastic achievement of students attending half-day sessions in the seventh grade. Unpublished research paper, University of Minnesota, Minneapolis.

Gallagher, J. J. (1960). *Analysis of research on the education of gifted children.* Springfield, IL: Office of the Superintendent of Public Instruction.

Gallagher, J. J. (1964). *Teaching the gifted child.* Boston: Allyn & Bacon.

Gallagher, J. J., & Coleman, M. R. (1992). *Cooperative learning survey.* Chapel Hill, NC: Gifted Education Policy Studies Program.

Gallagher, J. J., Coleman, M. R., & Nelson, S. M. (1983). *Cooperative learning as perceived by educators of gifted students and proponents of cooperative education.* Chapel Hill, NC: Gifted Education Policy Studies Program.

Gardner, J. (1983). *Frames of mind: the theory of multiple intelligences.* New York: Basic Books.

Gardner, H. (1993a). *Multiple intelligences: the theory in practice.* New York: Basic Books.

Gardner, H. (1993b). *Creating minds.* New York: Basic Books.

Gazzaniga, M. S. (1988). *Mind matters.* Boston: Hougton-Mifflin.

Getzels, J. W., & Jackson, P. W. (1962). *Creativity and intelligence.* New York: Wiley.

Goertzel, V., & Goertzel, M. (1962). *Cradles of eminence.* Boston: Little, Brown.

Goff, K., & Torrance, E. P. (1991). *Mentor's guide and protege's handbook.* Buffalo, NY: Bearly Limited.

Goleman, D. (1996). *Emotional intelligence.* Tucson, AZ: Zephyr Press.

Gordon, W. J. J. (1961). *Synectics: the development of creative capacity.* New York: Harper & Row.

Gordon, W. J. J. (1973). *The metaphorical way of knowing.* Cambridge, MA: Porpoise Books.

Gray, W. A. (1988). *Developing a planned mentoring program: principles and practices.* East Aurora, NY: D. O. K. Publishers.

Greenwood, C. R., Carta, J. J., & Kamps, D. (1990). Teacher-mediated versus peer-mediated instruction. A review of the advantages and disadvantages. In H. C. Foot, J. J. Morgan, & R. H. Slate (Eds.), *Children helping children.* New York: Wiley.

Gregorc, A. F. (1979). *Learning/teaching styles: diagnosing and prescribing programs.* Reston, VA: National Association of Secondary Schools Principals.

Gowan, J. C. (March 1958). Recent research on the education of gifted children. *Psychological Newsletter, 9*, 140-144.

Guilford, J. P. (1956). Structure of intellect. *Psychological Bulletin, 53*, 267-293.

Guilford, J. P. (1959). Three faces of intellect. *American Psychologist, 14*, 469-479.

Guilford, J. P. (1961). Factorial angles of psychology. *Psychological Review, 68*, 1-20.

Guilford, J. P. (1962a). What to do about creativity in education. In Conference Proceedings of the Educational Testing Service, Los Angeles: Educational Testing Service.

Guilford, J. P. (1962b). Factors that aid and hinder creativity. *Teachers College Record, 63*, 380-392.

Guilford, J. P. (1967a). *The nature of human intelligence*. New York: McGraw-Hill.

Guilford, J. P. (1967b). Creativity: yesterday, today, tomorrow. *Journal of Creative Behavior.* 1: 1-14.

Guilford, J. P. (1977). *Way beyond the I. Q.* Buffalo, NY: Bearly Limited.

Guilford, J. P. (1986). *Creative talents: their nature, uses and development*. Buffalo, NY: Bearly Limited.

Guilford, J. P., & Hoepfner, R. (1963). *Current structure factors and suggested tests*. Los Angeles: University of Southern California.

Haeger, W. W., & Feldhusen, J. F. (1989). *Developing a mentor program*. East Aurora, NY: D.O.K. Publisher.

Hansen, B. (1948). Sociodrama, a methodology for democratic methodology. *Sociatry, 2*, 347-362.

Hencley, S. P., & Yates, J. R. (1974). *Futurism in education: methodologies*. Berkeley, CA: McCutchan.

Herrmann, N. (1987). *The creative brain*. Lake Lure, NC: Brain Books.

Hirsch, S. (1979). Executive intern program. Report to the Office of Gifted and Talented, U. S. Office of Education, Washington, DC.

Hoch, O. (1962). Improving the present status of the creative student. *High School Journal, 46*, 14-22.

Hunt, J. McV. (1961). *Intelligence and experience*. New York: Ronald.

Hutchinson, W. L. (1961). *Creative and productive thinking in the classroom*. Doctoral dissertation, University of Utah, Salt Lake City, UT.

International Science Fair (1968). (September-October, 1968). *American Youth*, 17-19.

Janicek, A. (1993). Cooperative learning or ability grouping: A student's view. *TEMPO, Association for the Gifted, 12*, 1,9.

Johnson, D., & Johnson, R. (1991). What cooperative learning has to offer the gifted. *Cooperative Learning, 11*(3), 24-27.

Johnson, D., Johnson, R., & Holubic, E. J. (1990). *Choices of learning: cooperation in the classroom*. Edina, MN: Interaction Books.

Kelly, L. (1996). *Challenging minds: thinking skills and enrichment activities*. Waco, TX: Prufrock Press.

Klein, A. F. (1956). *Role playing in leadership training*. New York: Association Press.

Kolb, D. A. (1986). *The learning style inventory*. Boston: McBer & Co.

Kolb, D. A. (1988). *Experiential learning and the source of learning and development*. Englewood Cliffs, NJ: Prentice-Hall.

Kulik, J. A. (1992). *An analysis of the research on ability grouping: historical and contemporary perspectives*. Storrs, CT: National Research Center on the Gifted and Talented, University of Connecticut.

Kulik, J. A., Bangert, R. L., & Williams, C. W. (1983). Effects of computer-based teaching on secondary school students. *Journal of Educational Psychology, 75*, 19-26.

Kulik, J. A., & Kulik, C. (1987). Effects of ability grouping on achievement. *Equity and Excellence, 23*, 1-2, 22-30.

Kulik, J. A., & Kulik, C. (1991). Ability grouping and gifted students. In N. Colangelo & G. A. Davis (Eds.). *Handbook of gifted education*. Boston: Allyn & Bacon.

Lambert, S. E., & Lambert, J. W. (1982). Mentoring, a powerful learning device. *Gifted Children Today, 25*, 12-13.

Lazear, D. (1994a). *Seven pathways of learning: teaching students and parents about multiple intelligences*. Tucson, AZ: Zephyr Press.

Lazear, D. (1994b). *Multiple intelligence approach to assessment: solving the assessment conumdrum*. Tucson, AZ: Zephyr Press.

Lazear, D. (1996). *Step beyond your limits*. Tucson, AZ: Zephyr Press.

Lorge, I. (1945). Schooling makes a difference. *Teachers College Record, 46*, 483-492.

Lozanov, G. (1977). *Suggestology and suggestopedy*. New York: Gordon & Breach.

McCarthy, B. (1987). *The 4MAT system: teaching to learning style with right and left mode techniques*. Tucson, AZ: Zephyr Press.

McConnell, T. R. (1934). Discovery vs. authoritative identification in the learing of children. *University of Iowa Studies in Education, 9* (5), 13-62.

McKeachie, W. J. (1958). Motivating students' interest. In R. M. Cooper (Ed.). *The two ends of the log*, pp. 36-39. Minneapolis: University of Minnesota Press.

MacKinnon, D. W. (Ed.). (1961). *The creative person*. Berkeley: University of California Extension.

MacKinnon, D. W. (1986). *The assessment of personal effectiveness*. Buffalo, NY: Creative Education Foundation.

McPhee, D. M. (1996). *Limitless learning: an everyday event*. Tucson, AZ: Zephyr Press.

Maslow, A. H. (1954). *Motivation and personality*. New York: Harper & Row.

Mason, J. (1996). *Qualitative researching*. Thousand Oaks, CA: Sage Publications.

May, R. (1975). *The courage to create*. New York: W. W. Norton.

Meeker, M. (1969). *The structure of intellect: its interpretation and uses*. Columbus, OH: Merrill Publishers.

Millar, G. W. (1992). *Developing student questioning skills: a handbook of tips and strategies for teachers*. Bensenville, IL: Scholastic Testing Service.

Moore, O. K. (1961). Orthographic symbols and the pre-school child — a new approach. In E. P. Torrance (Ed.). *New educational ideas: the third Minnesota conference on gifted children*, pp. 91-101. Minneapolis: Center for Continuation Study, University of Minnesota.

Moreno, J. L. (1946). *Psychodrama. First volume*. Beacon, NY: Beacon House.

Moreno, J. L. (1952). Psychodramatic production techniques. *Group Psychotherapy, 4*, 243-273.

Moreno, J. L., Moreno, Z. T. (1969). *Psychodrama. Third volume*. Beacon, NY: Beacon House.

Moreno, Z. T. (1959). A survey of psychodramatic production techniques. *Group Psychotherapy and Psychodrama, 12*, 5-14.

Munari, B. (1957). *Who's there? Open the door*. New York: World.

Munari, B. (1959a). *The elephant's wish*. New York: World.

Munari, B. (1959b). *The birthday present*. New York: World.

Myers, R. E. (1994). *Facing the issues: creative strategies for probing social concerns*. Tucson, AZ: Zephyr Press.

Myers, R.E. (1996). *Cognitive connections: multiple ways of thinking with math*. Tucson, AZ: Zephyr Press.

Myers, R. E., & Torrance, E. P. (1994). *What next? futuristic scenarios for creative problem solving*. Tucson, AZ: Zephyr Press.

Nash, D., & Treffinger, D. (1993). *The mentor: A step by step guide to creating an effective mentor program in your school.* Waco, TX: Prufrock Press.

National Commission of Excellence in Education. (1983). *A nation at risk.* Washington, DC: U. S., Department of Education.

Nelson, M., Gallagher, J. J., & Coleman, M. R. (1993). Cooperative learning from two different perspectives. *Roeper Review, 16,* 117-121.

Neethling, K. (1993). *Creative people can perform miracles.* Pretoria: Benedic Books.

Neethling, K. (1994). *The courage to shake hands with tomorrow.* Pretoria: Benedic Books.

Noller, R. B., & Frey, B. R. (1995). *Mentoring for the continuing development of lost prizes.* In K. W. McCluskey, P. A. Baker, S. C. O'Hagan & D. J. Treffinger (Eds.), *Lost Prizes,* pp. 203-212. Sarasota, FL: Center for Creative Living.

Ojemann, R. H. (1948). Research in planned learning programs and the science of behavior. *Journal of Educational Research, 42,* 96-104.

Ojemann, R. H., Pritchett, K. (1963). Piaget and the role of guided experiences in human development. *Perceptual and Motor Skills, 17,* 927-939.

Ornstein, J. (February 1961). New recruits for science. *Parents Magazine, 36* (42), 101-103.

Ornstein, R. E. (Ed.). (1973). *The nature of human consciousness.* San Francisco: W. H. Freeman.

Osborn, A. F. (1963). *Applied imagination. (3rd. Ed.).* New York: Charles Scribner's.

Pankratz, L. D., & Buchan, G. (1965). Extended doubling and mirroring "in situ" in a mental hospital. *Group Psychotherapy and Psychodrama, 24,* 136-151.

Parnes, S. (1972). Creativity: Unlocking Human Potential. DOK Publishers: Buffalo, New York.

Parnes, S. (1975). Insights in Creative Behavior. *Aha: Insights Into Creative Behavior.* The Creative Education Foundation: Buffalo, New York.

Parnes, S. J. (1967). *Creative behavior guidebook.* New York: Charles Scribner's.

Parnes, S. J. (1981). *The magic of your mind.* Buffalo, NY: Bearly Limited.

Parnes, S. J. (1988). *Visioning: state-of-the-art processes for encouraging innovative excellence.* East, Aurora, NY: D. O. K. Publishers.

Parnes, S. J. (Ed.). (1992). *Source book for creative problem solving.* Buffalo, NY: Creative Education Press.

Passow, A. H. (1958). Enrichment of education for the gifted. In N. B. Henry (Ed.). *Education for the gifted,* pp. 193-221. (Fifty-seventh Yearbook, National Society for the Study of Education). Chicago: University of Chicago Press.

Peters, M. R. (1971). *A class divided.* Garden City, NY: Doubleday.

Pressey, S. L. (1954). The most misunderstood concept, acceleration. *School and Society, 79,* 59-60.

Raina, M. K. (1996). *Talent search in the third world.* New Delhi: Vikas Publishing House.

Reilly, J. (1992). *Mentorship: the essential guide for schools and business.* Dayton, OH: Ohio Psychological Press.

Reis, S. M., Burns, D., Renzulli, J. (1992). *Curriculum compacting: the complete guide for modifying the regular curriculum for high ability students.* Mansfield Center, CT: Creative Learning Press.

Reis, S. M., & Jordan, T. (1993). Using the talents unlimited model in enrichment programs. In C. L. Schlichter & W. R. Palmer (Eds.), *Thinking smart: a primer of the talents unlimited model,* pp. 119-140. Mansfield Center, CT: Creative Teaching Press.

Renzulli, J. S. (1977). *The enrichment triad model: a guide for developing defensible programs for the gifted and talented.* Mansfield Center, CT: Creative Learning Press.

Renzulli, J. S. (1979). What makes giftedness: a re-examination of the definition of gifted and talented. Ventura, CA: Ventura County Superintendent of Schools.

Renzulli, J. S. (1994). *Schools for talent development: A practical Plan for total school improvement*. Mansfield Center, CT: Creative Learning Press.

Renzulli, J. S., Reis, S. M., & Smith, L. H. (1981). *The revolving door identification model*. Mansfield Center, CT: Creative Learning Press.

Reynolds, M. C. (1960). Acceleration. In E. P. Torrance (Ed.), *Talent and education*, pp. 106-125. Minneapolis: University of Minnesota Press.

Richert, E. S. (1991). Rampant problems and promising practices in identification. In N. Colangelo & G. A. Davis (Eds.), *Handbook of gifted education*, pp. 61-96. Boston: Allyn & Bacon.

Richert, E. S., Alvino, J., & McDonnel, R. (1982). *The national report on identification: assessment and recommendations for comprehensive identification of gifted and talented youth*. Sewell, NJ: Educational Information and Resource Center, for the US Department of Education.

Roe, A. (1952). *The making of a scientist*. New York: Dodd, Mead.

Roe, A. (1960). Crucial life experiences in the development of scientists. In E. P. Torrance (Ed.), *Education and talent*, pp. 66-77. Minneapolis: University of Minnesota Press.

Roe, A. (1963). Personal problems and science. In C. W. Taylor & F. Barron (Eds.). *Scientific creativity: its recognition and development*, pp. 132-138. New York: Wiley.

Rose, L. (1996). *Developing intelligences through literature*. Tucson, AZ: Zephyr Press.

Rosenbloom, P. C. (Ed.). (1964). *Modern viewpoints in the curriculum*. New York: McGraw-Hill.

Runions, T. (1980). The mentor academy program: educating the gifted and talented for the 90's. *Gifted Child Quarterly*, *24*, 152-157.

Russell, S. J. & Corwin, R. B. (1989). *Statistics: The shape of the data. A unit of study for grades 4-6 from Used Data in the Classroom*. Palo Alto, CA: Dale Seymour Publications.

Schlichter, C. L. (1993). Talents unlimited: implementing the multiple talent approach in mainstream and gifted programs. In C. L. Schlichter & W. R. Palmer (Eds.), *Thinking smart: a primer of the talents unlimited model*, pp. 21-44. Mansfield Center, CT: Creating Press.

Schlichter, C. L., & Palmer, W. R. (1993). *Thinking smart: a primer of the talents unlimited model*. Mansfield Center, CT: Creative Teaching Press.

Schmeck, R. R. (Ed.). (1988). *Learning strategies and learning styles*. New York: Plenum.

Seely, K. (1985). Facilitators for the gifted learners. In J. E. Feldhusen (Ed.), *Toward excellence in gifted education*, pp. 105-133. Denver, CO: Lone Publishing.

Shallcross, D. J. (1981). Teaching Creative Behavior. Prentice Hall: Englewood Cliffs, New Jersey.

Shallcross, D. J., & Sisk, D. (1985). *The growing person*. Buffalo, NY: Bearly Limited.

Shane, H. G. (1960). Grouping in elementary school. *Phi Delta Kappa*, *40*, 313-318.

Shapiro, G. (1988). Teaching the gifted and talented teacher: a training model. *Gifted Child Quarterly*, *19*, 8-89.

Shepherd, J. (1972). Black lab power. *Saturday Review*, *55* (32), 32-39.

Shore, B., Cornell, D. G., Robinson, & Ward, V. S. (1991). *Recommended practices in gifted education: a critical analysis*. New York: Teachers College Press.

Shotka, J. (1961). Creative reading. *Education*, *82*, 26-28.

Showell, E. H. & Amram, F. B. (1995). *From Indian corn to outer space: Women invent in America*. Peterborough, NH: Cobblestone Publishing.

Silverman, L. (1995). Highly gifted children. In J. Genschalt, M. Birely, & C. Hollinger (Eds.), *Serving gifted and talented students*. Austin, TX: Pro-ed.

Silverman, L. & Kearney, K. (1992). The case for the Stanford-Binet LM as a supplemental test. *Roeper Review*, *5*, 34-37.

Simonton, D. K. (1990). *Psychology, science, and history: an introduction to historiometry.* New Haven, CT: Yale University Press.

Sisk, D. (1985). *Tomorrow's promise: how to encourage leadership in gifted students.* Atlanta, GA: Turner Broadcasting Company.

Sisk, D. (1987). *Creative teaching of the gifted.* New York: McGraw-Hill.

Sisk, D. (1993). *Systematic training of educational training of educational programs for underserved pupils (Project Step Up).* Washington, DC: U. S. Department of Education.

Sisk, D. & Rosselli, H. (1987). *Leadership: a special type of giftedness.* Monroe, NY: Trillium Press.

Sisk, D. A. & Shallcross, D. J. (1986). *Leadership: making things happen.* Buffalo, NY: Bearly Limited.

Sisk, D. & Whaley, C. (1987). *The futures primer for the classroom teachers.* Monore, NY: Trillium Press.

Skromme, A. B. (1989). *The 7-abilities plan.* Moline, IL: Self-Confidence Press.

Slavin, R. E. (1990). Research on cooperative learning: consensus and controversy. *Educational Leadership,* 52-54.

Slavin, R. E. (1991a). Are cooperative learning and "untracking" harmful to the gifted? Response to Allan. *Educational Leadership, 48* (6), 68-71.

Slavin, R. E. (1991b). What cooperative learning has to offer the gifted. *Cooperative Learning, 11* (3), 22-23.

Slavin, R. E., Madden, N. A., & Stevens, R. J. (1990). Cooperative learning models for the 3R's. *Educational Leadership,* 22-28.

Sloane, P. & MacHale, D. (1995). *Innprove your lateral thinking.* New York: Sterling Publishing Company.

Smith, M. R. (1950). The "silent" auxiliary ego technique in rehabilitating deteriorated mental patients. *Group Psychotherapy and Psychodrama, 3,* 92-100.

Spencer, L. M. (1957). Oklahoma identifies its talented youth. In *The Oklahoma science education story,* pp. 9-11. New York: Thomas Alva Edison Foundation.

Spitz, R. A. (1945). Hospitalism: an inquiry into the genesis of psychiatric condition in early childhood. *Psychoanalytic Studies of the Child, 1,* 53-74.

Spitz, R. A. (1946). Hospitalism: a follow-up report. *Psychoanalytic Studies of the Child, 2,* 113-117.

Stanish, B. (1977). *Sunflowering.* Carthage, IL: Good Apple.

Stanley, J. C. (1979). The case for extreme educational acceleration of intellectually brilliant youth. In J. C. Gowan, J. Khatena, & E. P. Torrance (Eds.), *Educating the ablest: a book of readings on the education of gifted children,* pp. 93-102. Itaska, IL: F. E. Peacock Publishers.

Stanley, J. C. & Benbow, C. P. (1986). Youths who reason exceptionally well mathematically. In R. J. Sternberg & J. E. Davidson (Eds.), *Conceptions of giftedness,* pp. 361-387. New York: Cambridge University Press.

Stein, M. I. (1974). *Stimulating creativity. Vol 1.* New York: Academic Press.

Sternberg, R. J. (1983). *How can we teach intelligence?* Philadelphia, PA: Research for Better Schools.

Sternberg, R. (1984). *Beyond IQ: the triarchic theory of human intellingence.* New York: Cambridge University Press.

Sternberg, R. J. (1988). *The triarchic mind: a new theory of human intelligence.* New York: Viking.

Stolurow, L. M. (September 3, 1962). Social impact of programmed instruction: aptitudes and abilities revisited. Paper presented at the Annual Convention of the American Psychological Association, St. Louis, Missouri.

Taylor, C. W. (1962). Who are the exceptionally creative? *Exceptional Children, 28,* 421-431.

Taylor, C. W. (Ed.). (1964a). *Creativity: progress and potential.* New York: McGraw-Hill.

Taylor, C. W. (May 1964b). Developing creative characteristics. *The Instructor, 5,* 99-100.

Taylor, C. W. (Ed.). (1964c). *Widening horizons of creativity.* New York: McGraw-Hill.

Taylor, C. W. (1993). Cultivating new talents: a way to reach the educationally deprived. In C. L. Schlichter & W. R. Palmer (Eds.), *Thinking smart: a primer of the talents unlimited model,* pp. 13.20. Mansfield Center, CT: Creative Teaching Press.

Terman, L. M. (1954). The discovery and encouragement of exceptional talent. *American Psychologist, 9,* 21-230.

Toeman, Z. (1948). The double situation in psychodrama. *Sociatry, 1,* 436-446.

Torrance, E. P. (Ed.). (1960). *Talent and education.* Minneapolis: University of Minnesota Press.

Torrance, E. P. (1961). Curriculum frontiers for elementary gifted pupil: flying monkeys and silent lions. *Exceptional Children, 28,* 119-127.

Torrance, E. P. (1962a). *Guiding creative talent.* Englewood Cliffs, NJ: Prentice-Hall.

Torrance, E. P. (1962b). Cultural discontinuities and the development of originality of thinking. *Exceptional Children, 29,* 2-13.

Torrance, E. P. (1963a). *Educational and the creative potential.* Minneapolis: Unversity of Minnesota Press.

Torrance, E. P. (1963b). The creative personality and ideal pupil. *Teachers College Record, 65,* 220-226.

Torrance, E. P. (1964). Education and creativity. In C. W. Taylor (Ed.), *Creativity: progress and potential,* 129-154. New York: McGraw-Hill.

Torrance, E. P. (1965a). *Rewarding creative behavior.* Englewood Cliffs, NJ: Prentice-Hall.

Torrance, E. P. (1965b). *Gifted children in the classroom.* New York: Macmillan.

Torrance, E. P. (1970). *Encouraging creativity in the classroom.* Dubuque, IA: William C. Brown.

Torrance, E. P. (1972a). Can we teach children to think more cratively? *Journal of Creative Behavior, 6,* 114-143.

Torrance, E. P. (1972b). The predictive validity of the Torrance tests of creative thinking. *Journal of Creative Behavior, 6,* 236-252.

Torrance, E. P. (1979). *The search for satori and creativity.* Buffalo, NY: Creative Education Foundation.

Torrance, E. P. (1981). Predicting the creative behavior of elementary school children (1958-1980) — and the teachers who made the difference. *Gifted Child Quarterly, 25,* 55-62.

Torrance, E. P. (1982). Growing up creatively gifted with learning disabilities. In W. M. Cruickshank, J. W. Lerner (Eds.), *Coming of age,* pp. 24-35. Syracuse, NY: Syracuse University Press.

Torrance, E. P. (1984). *Mentor relationships: How they aid creative achievement, endure, change, and die.* Buffalo, NY: Bearly Limited.

Torrance, E. P. (1988). *Style of learning and thinking.* Bensenville, IL: Scholastic Testing Service.

Torrance, E. P., & Arsan, K. (1963). Experimental studies of homogeneous groups for creative scientific tasks. In W. W. Charters, Jr. & N. L. Gage. (Ed.), *Readings in the social psychology of education,* 133-140. Boston: Allyn & Bacon.

Torrance, E. P., Goff, K., & Satterfield, N. B. (1996). *Mentoring in the culture of poverty.* Athens, GA: Georgia Studies of Creative Behavior.

Torrance, E. P., & Harmon, J. A. (1961). Effects of memory, evaluative, and creative reading sets on test performance. *Journal of Educational Psychology, 52,* 207-214.

Torrance, E. P., Murdock, M., & Fletcher, D. C. (1996). *Creative Problem Solving through role playing.* Pretoria: Benedic Books.

Torrance, E. P., & Myers, R. E. (1962a). Teaching gifted elementary pupils research concepts and skills. *Gifted Child Quarterly*, *6*, 1-16.

Torrance, E. P., Myers, R. E. (1962b). *Teaching gifted elementary pupils how to do research.* Minneapolis: Perceptive Publishing Company.

Torrance, E. P., & Myers, R. E. (1970). *Creative learning and teaching.* New York: Harper & Row.

Torrance, E. P., and Safter, H. T. (1990). *The incubation model of teaching.* Buffalo, NY: Bearly Limited.

Van Tassell-Baska, J. (1986). Acceleration. In C. J. Maker (Ed.), *Critical issues in gifted education: defensible programs for the gifted*, pp. 179-196. Rockville, MD: Pro-Ed.

Vernon, P. E. (1948). Changes in abilities from 14 to 20 years. *Advances in Science, 5*, 138.

Waldrop, S. C. (1993). Evaluating student development in the classroom: strategies for the classroom teacher. In C. L. Schlichter & W. R. Palmer (Ed.), *Thinking smart: a primer of the talents unlimited model*, pp. 199-213.

Wallgren, A., Wallgren, B., Persson, R., & Jorner, U. (1996). *Graphing statistics and data.* Thousand Oaks, CA: Sage Publications.

Ward, V. S., et al. (1962). *The gifted student: a manual for program improvement.* Atlanta: Southern Regional Education Board.

Wenger, W. (1987). *How to increase your intelligence.* East Aurora, NY: D. O. K. Publishers.

Wenger, W. (1992). *Beyond teaching and learning: boost your exam results with proven breakthrough technology.* Gaithersburg, MD: Project Renaissance.

Whitmore, J. (1980). *Giftedness, conflict and underachievement.* Boston: Allyn & Bacon.

Williams, F. E. (1972). *A total creativity program for individualizing and humanizing the learning process.* Englewood Cliffs, NJ: Educational Technology Publications.

Williams, L. V. (1983). *Teaching for the two sides of the brain.* Englewood Cliffs, NJ: Prentice-Hall.

Winebrenner, S. (1992). *Teaching gifted kids in the regular classroom: strategies and techniques every teacher can use to meet the academic needs of the gifted and talented.* Minneapolis: Free Spirit Publishing.

Witty, P. (Ed.). (1951). *The gifted child.* Boston: Heath.

Yablonsky, L. (1976). *Psychodrama: resolving emotional problems through role playing.* New York: Basic Books.

Yamamoto, K. (1964). Threshold of intelligence in academic achievement of highly creative students. *Journal of Experimental Education, 32*, 401-405.

Appendices

APPENDIX A

IDEAL CHILD CHECKLIST

Developed by E. Paul Torrance
Georgia Studies of Creative Behavior, College of Education
The University of Georgia — August 1967

Check all that apply:
__ Gifted Teacher   __ Elementary   __ Middle School   __ Secondary
__ Parent __ Coordinator/Consultant/Administrator __ University Personnel

What kind of person would you like the children you teach to become? Please try to describe the kind of person you would like for your pupils to become by using the checklist of characteristics on this sheet.
- Place one check by each of the characteristics you think is generally desirable and should be encouraged.
- Then place a second check by the characteristics you consider most important and should be encouraged above all others.
- Finally, draw a line through those characteristics you consider undesirable and usually discourage or punish.

__ 1. Adventurous, testing limits	__ 34. Never bored, always interested
__ 2. Affectionate, loving	__ 35. Obedient, submissive to authority
__ 3. Altruistic, working for good of others	__ 36. Persistent, persevering
__ 4. Asking questions about puzzling things	__ 37. Physically strong
__ 5. Attempting diflicult tasks	__ 38. Popular, well-liked
__ 6. Becoming preoccupied with tasks	__ 39. Preferring complex tasks
__ 7. Conforming	__ 40. Quiet, not talkative
__ 8. Considerate of others	__ 41. Receptive to ideas of others
__ 9. Courageous in convictions	__ 42. Refined, free of coarseness
__ 10. Courteous, polite	__ 43. Regressing occasionally, may be playful, childlike, etc.
__ 11. Competitive, trying to win	__ 44. Remembering well
__ 12. Critical of others	
__ 13. Curious, searching	__ 45. Reserved
__ 14. Desirous of excelling	__ 46. Self-assertive
__ 15. Determined, unflinching	__ 47. Self-confident
__ 16. Disturbing procedures and organization of the group	__ 48. Self-starting, initiating
	__ 49. Self-sufficient
__ 17. Doing work on time	__ 50. Sense of beauty
__ 18. Domineering, controlling	__ 51. Sense of humor
__ 19. Feeling emotions strongly	__ 52. Sincere, earnest
__ 20. Emotionally sensitive	__ 53. Socially well-adjusted
__ 21. Energetic, vigorous	__ 54. Spirited in disagreement
__ 22. Fault-finding, objecting	__ 55. Striving for distant goals
__ 23. Fearful apprehensive	__ 56. Stubborn, obstinate
__ 24. Guessing, hypothesizing	__ 57. Talkative
__ 25. Haughty and self-satisfied	__ 58. Thorough
__ 26. Healthy	__ 59. Timid, shy, bashful
__ 27. Independent in judgement	__ 60. Truthful; even when it hurts
__ 28. Independent in thinking	__ 61. Unsophisticated, artless
__ 29. Industrious, busy	__ 62. Unwilling to accept things on mere say-so
__ 30. Intuitive	__ 63. Versatile, well-rounded
__ 31. Liking to work alone	__ 64. Visionary, idealistic
__ 32. Neat and orderly	__ 65. Willing to accept judgements of authorities
__ 33. Negativistic, resistant	__ 66. Willing to take risks

APPENDIX B

SAMPLE OF TEN DEFINITIONS OF INCUBATION

This Appendix contains a sample of selected definitions of incubation by some of the leading scholars of the creative process. A much larger sample can be found in Torrance and Safter's (1990) The Incubation Model of Teaching.

Silvano Arieti, M.D.

As far as incubation is concerned, it is a well-known fact — even in simple learning — that a process of consolidation is necessary. For instance, students know that they cannot retain well what they have studied and learned just before taking a test, for instance, in early morning hours immediately preceding the examination. They must "sleep on" material. It could be that the material to be committed to memory must reverberate in the neuronal circuits, completely outside of consciousness, in order to make lasting connections.

Arieti, S. (1976). **Creativity: The magic synthesis.** NY: Basic Books, p. 19.

Richard S. Crutchfield

The word "incubate" comes from a Latin word meaning "to lie down" thus when we speak of "sleeping on a problem," we are, in effect, incubating. It is of interest also to note that in certain ancient Roman religious rites, incubation referred to a lying down on a mat in order to have dreams in which one communicated with certain deities of the underworld. The original meaning has suggestive metaphorical implications of our thinking about incubation in the creative process. The incubation process would seem to be one in which the individual somehow gets in touch with something mysterious, beyond what is available in his usual conscious life.

Crutchfield, R. S. (1973). In Bloomberg, M. (Ed.). **Creativity.** New Haven, CT: College & University Press, p.64.

Gary A. Davis

. . . incubation may best be viewed as a period of pre-conscious, fringe-conscious, off-conscious or perhaps even unconscious mental activity that takes place while the thinker is (perhaps deliberately) jogging, watching TV, playing golf, eating pizza, walking along a lakeshore, or even sleeping.

Davis, G. A. (1983, 1986). **Creativity is forever,** (2nd Ed.). Dubuque, IA: Kendall/Hunt, p. 62.

Jacob W. Getzels

The incubation period permits the operation of certain "unconscious" processes, the incubation period permits "unfreezing" of a fixated way of perceiving the problem and its elements, the incubation period permits the "retrieval" of information from memory storage, the incubation period permits the "transformation" of material that is memorized or perceived in established ways into novel patterns.

Getzels, J. W. (1975). Prospects and issues. In Taylor, I. A. & Getzels, J. W., **Perspectives in creativity,** Chicago, IL: Aldine, p. 339.

J. P. Guilford

Incubation means a period in the behavior of the individual during which there is no apparent activity on his part toward the solution of a problem, but during which or at the end of which there are definite signs of further attempts, with sometimes material progress toward a solution. During the interval the individual may have spontaneous glimpses of the activity. The period of incubation may be a matter of minutes or hours, even days, months, or years.

Guilford, J. P. (1979). Some incubated thoughts on incubation, *Journal of Creative Behavior,* 13 (1), 1-8, p. 1.

Ned Hermann

In the incubation stage, we step back from the problem and let our minds contemplate and work it through.

   Incubation . . . involves contemplation, subconscious processing, reflection, mulling visualization and sensory perception.

Hermann, N. (1987). **The creative brain,** Lake Lure, NC: Brain Dominance Institute, pp. 4, 7.

Michael LeBoeuf

Once you have immersed yourself with information, the next step is to let your right brain take over. Don't work on the problem. Forget about it. This period of incubation is where you allow your thoughts to go underground and put your subconscious to work.

   The incubation period may be long or short, but one thing is certain, it has to occur. Take a walk. Take a nap. Take a bath. Work on another project or hobby. Forget it for a week-end. Sleep on it.

Leboeuf, M. (1982). **Imagineering,** NY: McGraw-Hill, p. 58.

Alex F. Osborn

The part of the creative process that calls for little or no conscious effort is known as incubation. The root of that noun is a verb meaning "to lie down," thus it carries a connotation of purposive relaxation. . . . In its application to the workings of imagination, the terms covers the phenomenon by which ideas spontaneously well up into our consciousness.

Osborn, A. F. (1963). **Applied Imagination.** (3rd Ed.). NY: Charles Scribner's, p. 314.

D. N. Perkins

By definition, incubation occurs when time away from a problem helps to solve the problem. We often have the impression that this has happened when we set a stubborn problem aside and then think of a solution out of the blue, or immediately upon returning to the problem. It's important in considering incubation to keep separate the phenomenon and the explanations for it. The word incubation itself suggests that something is gradually developing, and sometimes people use the work as though it *meant* extended unconscious thinking. However, I want to emphasize that, as used in psychology, incubation means only that time away from a problem, helped, no matter how.

Perkins, D. N. (1981). **The mind's best work.** Cambridge, MA: Harvard University Press, p. 50.

Graham Wallas

The incubation stage covers two different things, of which the first is the negative fact that during incubation we do not voluntarily or consciously think on a particular problem, and the second is the positive fact that a series of unconscious and involuntary (or foreconscious and forevoluntary) mental events may take place during that period . . . the period of (voluntary) abstention may be spent either in conscious mental work or other problems, or in a relaxation from all conscious mental work.

Davis, G. A. (1983, 1986). **Creativity is forever.** (2nd Ed.). Dubuque, IA: Kendall/Hunt, pp. 62-63.

APPENDIX C

FORMS FOR OBTAINING GIFTED AND TALENTED NOMINATION FROM DIFFERENT SOURCES

The forms contained in this appendix were developed for use in Tampa, Florida for identifying gifted and talented students from parents, students, themselves, media specialists, art education specialists, physical education specialists, music educators, community workers, and school staffs.

PARENT NOMINATION FORM

Student Name_____ Grade_____ Date_____

Person completing this form_____

Relationship to child _____

(The following should be evident in quality beyond what is typical for the nominee's age/grade level.)

	HARDLY EVER (10% of the time)	SOME-TIMES (50-60% of the time)	OFTEN (75% of the time)
1. Asks a lot of questions.	_____	_____	_____
2. Tries to solve problems and figure things out.	_____	_____	_____
3. Has many ideas and a lot to say.	_____	_____	_____
4. Likes to make new things and/or tell stories.	_____	_____	_____
5. Amuses himself or herself.	_____	_____	_____
6. Solves problems in more than one way.	_____	_____	_____
7. Likes to pretend.	_____	_____	_____
8. Is sometimes bossy and may not always show interest in helping others.	_____	_____	_____
9. Can stay focused on a task for a long period of time.	_____	_____	_____
10. Can make good choices.	_____	_____	_____
11. Likes to be in school.	_____	_____	_____

INDIVIDUAL STUDENT NOMINATION FORM

Student Name_____ Grade_____ Date_____

Person completing this form_____

Relationship to child _____

(The following should be evident in quality beyond what is typical for the nominee's age/grade level.)

	HARDLY EVER (10% of the time)	SOME-TIMES (50-60% of the time)	OFTEN (75% of the time)
1. Asks a lot of questions.	_____	_____	_____
2. Displays a sense of humor; makes others laugh.	_____	_____	_____
3. Knows about things of which other children are unaware.	_____	_____	_____
4. Has area of special interest; collects things.	_____	_____	_____
5. Tends to dominate others.	_____	_____	_____
6. Understands abstract relationships.	_____	_____	_____
7. Has a holistic approach to problem solving.	_____	_____	_____
8. Demands an extraordinary amount of your time.	_____	_____	_____
9. Has a mathematical perception of the world (understands money).	_____	_____	_____
10. Challenges authority or adult opinions.	_____	_____	_____
11. Gives the teacher "that feeling" that he/she is gifted.	_____	_____	_____

STUDENT SELF-NOMINATION FORM

Student Name _____ Grade _____ Date _____

Your Teacher's Name _____

	HARDLY EVER (10% of the time)	SOME-TIMES (50-60% of the time)	OFTEN (75% of the time)
1. I'm a good guesser.	_____	_____	_____
2. I have a sense of humor; I can make others laugh.	_____	_____	_____
3. I have friends that are smart.	_____	_____	_____
4. I can get other people to do things I want them to do.	_____	_____	_____
5. I like to boss people around.	_____	_____	_____
6. I get in trouble for asking too many questions.	_____	_____	_____
7. I have friends that are older than me.	_____	_____	_____
8. I am not afraid to try new things.	_____	_____	_____
9. I am told that I have a good imagination.	_____	_____	_____
10. I like to find out how things work.	_____	_____	_____
11. I like to daydream.	_____	_____	_____

MEDIA SPECIALIST EDUCATION NOMINATION FORM

Student Name _____Grade_____Date _____

Person completing this form_____

(The following should be evident in quality beyond what is typical for the nominee's age/grade level).

	HARDLY EVER (10% of the time)	SOME-TIMES (50-60% of the time)	OFTEN (75% of the time)
1. Spends a great amount of time reading and studying; checks out a lot of books.	_____	_____	_____
2. Very interested in books.	_____	_____	_____
3. Aware of details and descriptions, spontaneous categories.	_____	_____	_____
4. Works in an absorbed manner for lengthy periods of time.	_____	_____	_____
5. Persists in asking questions about a problem or a topic; reads a lot of books, articles on a topic.	_____	_____	_____
6. Follows up class activities by reading and/or researching	_____	_____	_____
7. Asks many intelligent questions about topics in which children do not normally have an interest.	_____	_____	_____
8. Has a wide range of reading.	_____	_____	_____
9. Has an avid interest in the areas of science or literature.	_____	_____	_____
10. Shows love of reading; is interested in all written material.	_____	_____	_____
11. Gives the teacher "that feeling" that he/she is gifted.	_____	_____	_____

ART EDUCATION NOMINATION FORM

Student Name _____ Grade _____ Date _____

Person completing this form_____

(The following should be evident in quality beyond what is typical for the nominee's age/grade level).

	HARDLY EVER (10% of the time)	SOME-TIMES (50-60% of the time)	OFTEN (75% of the time)
1. Uses materials in new and different ways.	_____	_____	_____
2. Learns quickly; grasps and applies techniques.	_____	_____	_____
3. Show mature spatial ability; organizes objects and materials in space.	_____	_____	_____
4. Is good at detailed work.	_____	_____	_____
5. Shows originality in ideas.	_____	_____	_____
6. Shows mature depth of field and perspective in drawings, paintings, and sculpture.	_____	_____	_____
7. Enjoys art; tends to expand on basic instructions.	_____	_____	_____
8. Likes to do "own thing" rather than follow instructions.	_____	_____	_____
9. Has a greater depth, more complete understanding of subject matter.	_____	_____	_____
10. Shows an advanced skill in a particular area of art.	_____	_____	_____
11. Gives the teacher "that feeling" that he/she is gifted.	_____	_____	_____

PHYSICAL EDUCATION NOMINATION FORM

Student Name _____ Grade_____ Date _____

Person completing this form_____

(The following should be evident in quality beyond what is typical for the nominee's age/grade level).

	HARDLY EVER (10% of the time)	SOME-TIMES (50-60% of the time)	OFTEN (75% of the time)
1. Learns quickly; grasps rules of a game quickly; has good memory for movement.	_____	_____	_____
2. Will argue; becomes very upset at supposed inequalities in a game.	_____	_____	_____
3. Tries for perfection; spends time to develop his/her skills; stays with it.	_____	_____	_____
4. Has many interests; likes to try new games.	_____	_____	_____
5. Shows good hand-eye/ foot-eye coordination; has skilled body movements.	_____	_____	_____
6. May have more advanced motor ability for his/her age.	_____	_____	_____
7. Has a great desire to excel, even to the point of cheating.	_____	_____	_____
8. Innovates; may make-up own games or new rules to an existing game; may use materials in a way other than intended.	_____	_____	_____
9. Others may look to this person for direction; persuades, organizes and influences others.	_____	_____	_____
10. May seem bossy with others gets impatient when others do not seem to understand the rules.	_____	_____	_____
11. Gives the teacher "that feeling" that he/she is gifted.	_____	_____	_____

MUSIC EDUCATION NOMINATION FORM

Student Name _____ Grade _____ Date _____

Person completing this form_____

(The following should be evident in quality beyond what is typical for the nominee's age/grade level).

	HARDLY EVER (10% of the time)	SOME-TIMES (50-60% of the time)	OFTEN (75% of the time)
1. Performs at sight (reading).	_____	_____	_____
2. Responds quickly to training.	_____	_____	_____
3. Displays exceptional talent or voice or instrument.	_____	_____	_____
4. Plays "by ear" or sings on first or second hearing.	_____	_____	_____
5. Plays more than one instrument.	_____	_____	_____
6. Improvises or innovates on instrument or voice.	_____	_____	_____
7. Perseveres in music.	_____	_____	_____
8. Is committed to music for long term.	_____	_____	_____
9. Becomes absorbed in music (performing or listening).	_____	_____	_____
10. Works toward perfection.	_____	_____	_____
11. Gives the teacher "that feeling" that he/she is gifted.	_____	_____	_____

COMMUNITY NOMINATION FORM

Student Name_____ Grade_____ Date_____

Person completing this form_____

Relationship to child _____

(The following should be evident in quality beyond what is typical for the nominee's age/grade level.)

	HARDLY EVER (10% of the time)	SOME-TIMES (50-60% of the time)	OFTEN (75% of the time)
1. Is able to remember and tell detailed information about happenings at school or in the neighborhood.	_____	_____	_____
2. Seems to know a lot about a lot of things.	_____	_____	_____
3. Questions authority; will argue; gets upset when he/she feels things are unfair.	_____	_____	_____
4. Knows what is going on; understands what is really happening in situations.	_____	_____	_____
5. Is frank in appraisal of adults or situations.	_____	_____	_____
6. Has a mature sense of humor.	_____	_____	_____
7. Tends to be prepared for early independence and survival.	_____	_____	_____
8. Tells imaginative stories.	_____	_____	_____
9. Asks lots of questions	_____	_____	_____
10. Frequently interrupts others when they are talking.	_____	_____	_____
11. Is resourceful and can solve problems by ingenious methods.	_____	_____	_____

SCHOOL STAFF NOMINATION FORM

Student Name_____ Grade_____ Date_____

Person completing this form_____

(The following should be evident in quality beyond what is typical for the nominee's age/grade level.)

	HARDLY EVER (10% of the time)	SOME-TIMES (50-60% of the time)	OFTEN (75% of the time)
1. Is a good guesser.	_____	_____	_____
2. Displays a sense of humor; makes others laugh; tells jokes.	_____	_____	_____
3. Is involved in many school activities.	_____	_____	_____
4. Has the ability to influence others, positively or negatively.	_____	_____	_____
5. Tends to dominate others.	_____	_____	_____
6. Asks a lot of questions.	_____	_____	_____
7. Shows self-confidence.	_____	_____	_____
8. Is a risk taker.	_____	_____	_____
9. Has a good imagination.	_____	_____	_____
10. Thinks of alternative ways to do things.	_____	_____	_____
11. Gives you "that feeling" that he/she is gifted.	_____	_____	_____

APPENDIX D

WAYS OF INDIVIDUALIZING INSTRUCTION TO USE RESOURCES OUTSIDE OF THE CLASSROOM

MENTORS

The use of mentors is an excellent resource for helping meet the special needs for gifted and talented children and youth which cannot be met in the classroom. This resource has been discussed in Chapter 13. If your school has a mentoring program the teacher can arrange for a mentor through this. However, this is not necessary. The teacher may know just the person who would be happy to serve as a mentor for such a student. Chambers of Commerce and some civic clubs have such programs. For example Athens, Georgia, has a Black Men Mentoring Black Boys Club which has been highly successful in helping boys who were unmotivated, failing in school, delinquent, and ready to drop out. Through a mentor many such boys have been helped to become highly motivated, avoid dropping out and delinquency, and achieve academically. At times, some of them emerge as gifted or talented.

Mentoring has been especially effective with students who are living in poverty. Many helpful suggestions have been given by Torrance, Goff, and Satterfield (1996) in the book *Mentoring in the Culture of Poverty*.

INDIVIDUAL OR SMALL GROUP RESEARCH PROJECTS

The development of research concepts and skills has been described and discussed in Chapter 11. After such a foundation has been developed, gifted and talented children are prepared to carry out research projects as individuals and as small groups. The use of research projects are also discussed by Renzulli (1977) in *The Enrichment Triad Model* and by Renzulli, Reis, and smith (1981) in *The Revolving Door Identification Model*.

SELF-DIRECTED LEARNING

Hazel Feldhusen (1993) in her book, *Individualized Teaching of Gifted Children in the Regular Classroom*, discusses the use of self-directed learning and learning agreements which may be used with the entire regular classroom or with individual gifted and talented students whose needs are not being met in the classroom. Self-directed learning provides many options such as time for reading books in the school library; writing in their individual journals, creative writing, and the like. Favorite activities of gifted and talented children are writing poetry, small books, dramas, advertisements, science fiction, and other kinds of short stories. Proof reading should be stressed.

SCHOOL LIBRARY

In addition to providing time in the school library, there are many other ways that both the school library and the community library may be used as a resource. School librarians, media specialists, and computer specialists can be used. If your classroom is not equipped with computers, this is the best opportunity to give gifted and talented children computer skills.

In today's world computer skills are essential for gifted and talented students. They should also be helped to use primary resources. Students may have to make use of public and university libraries.

FIELD TRIPS

Field trips provide exciting opportunities for gifted and talented children to fulfill needs that cannot be met in the classroom. Hazel Feldhusen (1993) points out the following advantages of such experiences (p. 40):

1. Visual, concrete experiences with phenomena they are studying.
2. A chance to explore and discover concepts and relationships in the real world.
3. Opportunity to learn new ideas about things outside the classroom.
4. Career education experiences.

When the whole class is involved, Feldhusen suggests that gifted and talented children be prepared through extended reading experiences for the field trip and to expect greater depth in their projects after the field trip. They might be given several books to read before the field trip. For field trips to be successful, it requires careful planning and they should have hands-on experiences and not simply walk through.

PUZZLES

Slone and MacHale (1995) have compiled a collection of puzzles designed to improve lateral thinking skills (de Bono, 1970). They can be used by an entire class, individually, in groups of two, or in small groups. In order to solve these puzzles, the students have to break away from conventional, dead-end assumptions and approach things from a new angle. The challenge is to find a logical explanation for what appears to be an illogical situation.

Using lateral thinking skills against these perplexing problems is fun and a rewarding way to improve lateral thinking skills. A special clue section provides hints for those who are stumped. Working on these puzzles can become an exciting game.

FUTURE PROBLEM SOLVING PROGRAM

The Future Problem Solving Program is a year-long curriculum project with competitive and non-competitive options. It has local, statewide, national, and international competitive programs. There is a new curriculum each year, consisting of two practice problems, a state Bowl program, and a national-international bowl problem. There is a primary division which is noncompetitive, an elementary division (grades 4-6), an intermediate division (grades 7-9), and a senior division (grades 10-12).

There are several components which provide options: group problem solving (4-5), individual problem solving, community problem solving, and scenario writing. It can be used in an entire classroom and as an out-of-class program. The out-of-class option may be directed by the teacher, a parent, or some other interested adult. Participants collect information about the problem, analyze the problem, and follow the process described in Chapter 6.

Program materials and information may be obtained from state or national-international directors. The national-international office may be reached at the following address:

Director, Future Problem Solving Program
2500 Packard Rd., Suite 110, Ann Arbor, MI 48104-6827 USA

ODYSSEY OF THE MIND

Odyssey of the Mind is the most popular of the national and international competitions. It also involves a large number of kinds of giftedness and talents — construction, invention, drama, writing, speech, mathematics, and science. It has typically been an out-of-class activity and is coached by parents, teachers, or other adults. The curriculum and program materials are carefully prepared and changed each year. For example, the problems for 1992-1993 were: Pit Stop, Dinosaurs, The Old Man of the Sea Analogy, Which End Is Up?, Folk Tales, and Li'l Gourmet.

The founder of the program is Samuel Micklus and the problems have always been designed to develop creative problem solving skills in all of the modalities in which creativity is expressed. The program has received much support from large corporations and a number of scholarships are awarded each year for performance. It is worldwide in scope. Its goals are reflected in the OM Pledge: "Let me be a seeker of knowledge, let me travel uncharted paths, and, let the world be a better place in which to live."

Problems, program materials, books, and other information may be obtained from:

> Creative Competitions, Inc.
> P. O. Box 27
> Glassboro, NJ 08028

INVENT AMERICA

A relatively new program (Project XL, 1989), Invent America has been developed by the U. S. Patent Model Foundation and designed to help children learn to develop their creativity, ingenuity, and motivation. Students participate by creating inventive solutions to problem needs in school, in the community, or at home with parent and teacher support. The competition begins at the local school level and culminates with the winners being presented patents in Washington, D. C. For more information contact: U.S. Patent Model Foundation, 1331 Pennsylvania Avenue, Suite 903, Washington, D. C. 20004.

OTHER COMPETITIONS

YOUNG GAME INVENTORS CONTEST

Children who are not more than 13-years old and who like to play and invent games, will find the *Young Game Inventors Contest* of great interest. The purpose is to provide young students an opportunity to apply their creativity by inventing a board game. Entries are judged for fun and creative ideas. The grand prize winner receives a four night, expenses-paid trip for three to San Francisco, the chance to have the game manufactured by University Games, and much more. For detailed information, contact Young Game Inventors Contest, U.S. Kids, P. O. Box 567, Indianapolis, IN 46206.

NOTE: We are indebted to Drs. Frances Karnes and Tracy Riley for the following activities. "Competitions: Developing and nurturing talents." *Gifted Child Today Magazine, 19*(2), 14-15, 49, 1996.

YOUNG AMERICAN PATRIOTIC ART AWARD

Through the Young American Creative Patriotic Art Awards, high school students express their artistic talents and demonstrate their patriotism while becoming eligible for funds to further their art education. Students may use water color, pencil, pastel, charcoal, tempera, crayon, acrylic, pen, and ink, or oil on paper or canvas in their entries. These are judged on originality of concept, patriotism expressed, content and clarity of ideas, design, use of color, technique, and total impact or execution and contrast. Awards include: $3,000 first prize; $2,000 second prize; $1,500 third prize; $1,000 fourth prize; and $500 fifth prize. The first prize also includes an expenses-paid weekend to the American Academy of Achievement and an expense paid trip to be honored at the next Veterans of Foreign Wars Auxiliary National Convention. For more information write Ladies Auxiliary to the Veterans of Foreign Wars, 406 W. 34th St., Kansas City, MO 64111.

NATIONAL TEEN BUSINESS PLAN COMPETITION

To give teens an opportunity to increase their understanding of the concepts, tools, and responsibilities of business ownership while putting their own entrepreneurial dreams on paper, the *National Teen Business Plan Competition* was established. Boys and girls who are 13 to 19 years old may apply. Entries are judged on the quality of the business plan. Five female and five male winners receive a trip to a major U. S. city for the next national competition. The winners also receive a resource kit of products and services. Furthermore, they are matched with business owners who act as business coaches by providing additional support and follow-up to the youngsters' exploration of business and entrepreneurship. For more information, contact: *National Teen Business Plan Competition*, An Income of Her Own, P. O. Box 987, Santa Barbara, CA 93102.

THE KIDS HALL OF FAME

Students who have made or are making a positive difference for themselves, their family, school, community, state, country, or world should know about *The Kid's Hall of Fame*. Students must be 14 years old or younger. Five national grand prize winners will each receive a $10,000 post-high school educational scholarship and a trip to Washington, DC for themselves and two parents or guardians. Twenty-five first prize winners each receive a $100 U. S. Savings Bond. For more information, contact: *The Kid's Hall of Fame* by Pizza Hut, P. O. Box 92477, Libertyville, IL 60092.

GUIDEPOST YOUNG WRITERS CONTEST

For those writers in your school, the *Guideposts Young Writers Contest* was developed to promote young people's writing talent and their awareness of how faith plays a part in their everyday lives. High school juniors and seniors or homeschooled students equivalent to these grades may enter. The first prize winner receives a $6,000 scholarship; second prize, a $5,000 scholarship; third prize, a $4,000 scholarship, and fourth through eighth prize, $1,000 scholarships each. The ninth through 25th prize winners receive a portable electronic typewriter. Scholarships are designated for the colleges or schools of the winner's choice. To get information, write *Guideposts Young Writers Contest, Guideposts Magazine*, 16 E. 34th St., New York, NY 10016.

DEBATE

Debating skills are of special interest to children and youth with gifts or talents in oratory, politics, speechmaking, and television performances. Special coaching may be given by parents, mentors, or other adults. Research, practice and coaching may take place outside of the classroom, but the debate might be brought back to the classroom or school.

Excellent suggestions for developing debating skills are given by Lynne Kelly (1996) in her book, *Challenging Minds*.

Subject Index

Name Index